The Law Firm Associate's Guide to

Personal Marketing and Selling Skills

Catherine Alman MacDonagh ■ Beth Marie Cuzzone

Contributing Author, Jim Hassett, Ph.D.

Commitment to Quality: The Law Practice Management Section is committed to quality in our publications. Our authors are experienced practitioners in their fields. Prior to publication, the contents of all our books are rigorously reviewed by experts to ensure the highest quality product and presentation. Because we are committed to serving our readers' needs, we welcome your feedback on how we can improve future editions of this book.

Cover design by Andrew Alcala, ABA Publishing.

Printed in the United States of America.

Library of Congress Cataloging-in-Publication Data

Alman MacDonagh, Catherine.

The law firm associate's guide to personal marketing and selling skills/By Catherine Alman MacDonagh and Beth Marie Cuzzone.—1st ed.

p. cm.

Includes index.

ISBN-13: 978-1-59031-830-0

1. Lawyers—United States—Marketing. 2. Advertising—Lawyers—United States. 3. Practice of law—United States. I. Cuzzone, Beth Marie. II. Title.

KF316.5.A95 2007

340.068'8—dc22

2007020518

09 08 07 5 4 3 2 1

I dedicate this to my wonderful children,
Alexander and Sarah.
You are the lights of my life.

—CAM

Dedicated to my inspiration—Kenna Marie.

—BMC

ABOUT THE AUTHORS

Photo by Tracy Powell

Beth Marie Cuzzone and
Catherine Alman MacDonagh

Beth Marie Cuzzone and **Catherine Alman MacDonagh, J.D.,** help lawyers and law firms grow their businesses and revenues. They are both recognized as innovators and industry leaders and have many of the same achievements from Legal Marketing Association board positions to national awards and honors such as *Boston Business Journal*'s 40 Under 40, LMA's *Your Honor Awards,* and *Marketing the Law Firm*'s MLF Top 50 List.

They are cofounders of the Legal Sales and Service Organization, Inc. (www.legalsales.org), the industry's only organization exclusively focued on sales, service and quality issues. Catherine and Beth, certified Six Sigma green belts, provide marketing and sales strategies, planning, and initiatives to their law firms. They enjoy publishing and speaking.

Beth, Director of Business Development at Goulston & Storrs PC, is known for her "first to market" initiatives. Prior to working in law firms, Beth was a consultant to a variety of organizations, including law firms and corporate legal departments, non-profits and educational entities. Beth is a trained facilitator and resides outside Boston with her husband and daughter.

Catherine is a former corporate counsel and a member of the New Jersey and New York bars, and the American Bar Association (Law Practice Management Section, Women Rainmakers, Strategic Marketing Group). She has developed groundbreaking client development initiatives as well as innovative training and coaching programs. Catherine brings more than 15 years of experience to her Director of Business Development position at Day Pitney LLP. She lives near Boston with her husband and two children.

ACKNOWLEDGMENTS

We could not and did not write this book without the help of many—our families, our friends, our colleagues, our mentors, and our law firms.

First, and foremost, thank you to everyone in our families for your unconditional love and encouragement in all that we do.

We are deeply grateful for the support of our many friends and colleagues, all of whom have contributed to this book and our lives in so many ways. If we thanked everyone individually, it might fill this book.

Heartfelt thanks to our contributing author, Jim Hassett, Ph.D., who helped shaped this book and the accompanying training manual.

Thank you to everyone who took extra time to share feedback, ideas, work, books, speeches, articles, and research, especially: Our friends at American Lawyer Media, Lynn Baronas, J.D., Larry Bodine, Hollis R. Chase, Silvia L. Coulter, Ronna West Cross, Esq., Bill Flannery, J.D., David H. Freeman, J.D., the Legal Sales and Service Organization Team, Suzanne Lowe, Roberta Montafia, Esq., Kathleen B. Patton, J.D., Michael Rynowecer, Marcie Borgal Shunk, and Dennis Snow.

We also recognize the law firms that are such important parts of our personal and professional lives.

Finally, we are indebted to Heather Jefferson, Beverly A. Loder, and Deborah McMurray, without whom this book would not have been published by the American Bar Association.

—Beth and Catherine

Special thanks and deep appreciation to my family: my parents, Sondra Sable Alman Gibbons and Richard D. Alman, for their constant love; Colin P. MacDonagh, with whom I share life's two greatest treasures and more . . . our children, Sarah and Alex, who mean more than anything in the universe, however large it may be; my sister, Susan Alman Schneider, and Barry, Margot, Joanna, and Amelia Schneider; and all my relatives (long live The Yetta Bowl!). With love forever, thanks to my sister, D. Lynn Alman, R.N., whom I miss so much. "Ripple in still water. . . ."

For extraordinary friendship and support, I thank: the American Foundation for Suicide Prevention; Silvia L. Coulter; Sara Ann Crocker; Ronna West Cross, Esq.; John O. Cunningham, Esq.; the marketing and business development team at Day, Berry & Howard LLP; Nan Myerson Evans, Esq.; Robert D. Greenbaum; the Legal Marketing Association (with special thanks to the New England Chapter); the Legal Sales and Service Organization; Roberta Montafia, Esq.; Ramona Montecarlo; Alyssa Napoleon; Norfolk *CARE*; Robert D. Randolph, Jr., Esq.; Ruberto, Israel & Weiner, P.C.; Self Esteem Boston; Kristin Diotalevi, Dawn Novak and everyone at Stella Dieci; Kristin T. Sudholz; and Jeffrey Weisenfreund.

—Catherine M. Alman MacDonagh

My family—John, Kenna, Pat, Gina, Clay, Zack, Nina, and Nick—a special thank you with love. I also want to recognize my extended family: The Corbett, O'Donnell, O'Malley, and Valerie families. I am also grateful to work with the legal industry's finest, the team at Goulston & Storrs, and I thank you for allowing me the opportunity to write this book.

—Beth Marie Cuzzone

In loving memory of
Lynn Alman

CONTENTS

ABOUT THIS BOOK

Time is a lawyer's stock and trade. We thank you for purchasing this book and for investing your time by reading it. Our pledge is to provide you with a readable guide that delivers a substantial return on your investment.

The Law Firm Associate's Guide to Personal Marketing and Selling Skills is for lawyers in any sized firm or practice area who understand that developing marketing and selling skills is not a luxury. Rather, it's a necessity for anyone who wants to be successful.

Lawyers believe that they have a unique challenge in marketing and selling their professional services and, in some respects, we agree. However, we know that these skills can be taught and learned, that they are required of anyone in any business, and that they are transferable in nature. You can (and in fact must) use personal marketing and selling skills to be successful anywhere. The earlier you develop good practices and incorporate them into your day, so that they become habitual, the better.

Our work and this book are based on a mission about which we are passionate—helping lawyers grow: professionally, personally, in their business, and in their relationships, especially with clients. The ideas and practical advice we provide in this Guide and accompanying Training Manual are based on our years of experience working with many lawyers, practicing law and being clients of lawyers and law firms.

One of the things we aim to do is change any negative perceptions or feelings you might have about "sales." In the context of selling and providing professional services, it is really about helping people, a reason many lawyers went to law school in the first place. And, speaking of law school, you probably didn't have a chance to take a class that focused on building your business, since most schools still (surprisingly) don't offer courses that even begin to touch on the subjects contained in this book.

Your personal marketing and selling skills are just that—YOURS. There is no one style or technique that is more suitable than another—it's very individual. So don't worry. We are not going to suggest that you fundamentally change who you are or that you should be disingenuous. Quite the opposite is true. We also won't recommend engaging in activities that you find terrifying or excruciating. We will, however, ask you to continuously develop and grow. And that means constantly stretching beyond your comfort zone. You must! We promise that, as with any learned activity, the new skills will become second nature with repetition and consistent effort.

As we were writing this book, we were introduced to a valuable working tool for lawyers: *Legal Business Development: A Step by Step Guide* by Jim Hassett, Ph.D. (self-published, 2006). Jim generously agreed to collaborate with us and shared his insights and materials. His contributions have been incorporated throughout the book and training manual. His advice is sure to help lawyers who are ready to commit to a marketing and business development program to realize their goals.

This book encompasses a breadth of knowledge from many industry thought leaders. It contains best practices and the kind of advice that you can easily adopt into your day-to-day business activities. Good business development and client retention comes from good habits.

The tips and techniques in this book are broken down by stages of the marketing cycle and stages of personal selling. This is intended to show how the processes and skills build on each other and all work together. When you follow them, you'll achieve success.

So don't delay, please start reading.

—CAM and BMC

FOREWORD

by Deborah McMurray

"Life is difficult." So said M. Scott Peck, M.D., in his worldwide bestselling book *The Road Less Traveled.* However, the professional life of an associate in a law firm doesn't have to be–at least when it comes to marketing and business development.

Like *The Road Less Traveled,* this is a book about simple things–steps associates can take to keep track of people they know, to support their friends and colleagues, and to set achievable goals and get closer to them every day. This book dispels commonly held myths about rainmaking and sales: (1) that it is someone else's job, (2) that all one needs to do is focus on technical proficiency and clients will come, (3) that there is a "rainmaking personality" and those scant few who have it are the only ones who can sell, and (4) that it doesn't matter to you because you don't plan on staying around to make partner anyway.

This is the first volume in the ABA's new groundbreaking Law Firm Associate's Development Series, created to teach key skills that associates and other lawyers need to succeed at their firms, but that they may not have learned in law school. While the context of the advice given here is what one should do when working in a law firm, the suggestions should be taken and held as "life lessons" for whatever path your career takes.

Catherine MacDonagh and Beth Cuzzone have built their successful legal marketing and sales careers by giving practical counsel that works. They aren't shy about sharing their advice and opinions, and this is one of the many reasons that they are sought after as advisors and colleagues.

There is no magic in the guidance they give lawyers, no recipe for secret sauce. The book is simply a compendium of tried and true blocking and tackling tools, accompanied by their collective years of knowing what works and what doesn't.

What more could a reader ask for?

Deborah McMurray
ABA Law Practice Management Section Author
CEO and Strategy Architect, Content Pilot LLC

INTRODUCTION

OVERVIEW

The practice of a law firm is no longer simply a profession—it's a business. The business of providing legal services today takes place in a competitive, fast-paced, ever-changing industry. Now, more than ever, lawyers must pay attention to client acquisition, service, and retention in order to compete and survive.

Associates in firms of all sizes have an important role to play in this business. Just as it is important to build technical skills, associates should learn about—as well as be trained and mentored in—marketing and business development. They must begin to develop the attendant abilities as early in their careers as possible.

Whether your plan is to grow a solo or small practice, become a partner in a large law firm, find an in-house position, or pursue an alternative career, the business skills you will learn in this book will apply regardless of your path. What you learn will help you be successful.

But let's get something clear right at the beginning—your success is up to YOU. Simply reading this book will not get you there; it merely provides you with a roadmap and some knowledge that gives you the potential for getting there. We've provided information and ideas that are actionable, but we can't do it for you, just like no one can study, diet, exercise, or floss for you.

HONING YOUR CRAFT

In the first few years of practice, there is wisdom in the more traditional emphasis on honing your craft. It is still imperative that you are knowledgeable. But it's abundantly clear that being a smart, technically-proficient lawyer isn't enough. There are plenty of those lawyers around, but what makes you different? How can prospects distinguish you from anyone else they might be considering?

We believe that being a terrific lawyer includes taking charge of your professional direction, being proactive about achieving your goals, and, of course, understanding what your *clients* think is important.

Whether you interface directly with clients or view the partners and other lawyers with whom you are working as your clients, relationships are paramount. Learning how to develop and maintain relationships is at the heart of sales, service, and, ultimately, your success. This requires skills that are just as important to develop as legal research, writing, and advocacy. A wise associate will quickly realize that providing excellent client service, in its broadest sense, is the key to a successful career.

We asked Lynn Baronas, J.D., Director of Professional Development and Diversity at Day Pitney LLP about why client service is so important for associates. Her answer was: A first-year associate begins to practice client service the moment he steps through the law firm door–as he routinely delivers quality substantive work product efficiently and on time, as he repeatedly demonstrates a first-rate work ethic, and as he intentionally cultivates his internal and external community connections. New lawyers who diligently practice and hone these basic "lawyering" skills simultaneously equip themselves to understand and deliver upon client goals and objectives. Over time, they grow into seasoned, senior lawyers who draw and retain clients.

The better an associate becomes at delivering excellent service, the more likely he is to move up tier quickly in complexity of work as well.

FINDING BALANCE

Today's associates demand more than a high salary and all the perks. They want balance–they want to have a career and live their lives too. Combine that with the fact that most associates don't always have control over their own time, don't always receive training outside of substantive areas, and may not be encouraged to focus on marketing and business development. It all adds up to more than a small potential for delays in taking actions today that will result in future benefits.

So often we hear from even the most seasoned lawyers that there just isn't enough time for all this "extra" marketing and sales stuff. Until times are slow. Then, they tend to express regret in the form of "if they had known then what they know now, they would have made the time to stay in touch with their network" type comments. This book is designed to help you avoid being in that position.

If you are you wondering how you will find the time to learn the art and science of rainmaking, the answer is simple. You must *make* the time. In today's competitive climate, you really don't have a choice. Be the captain of your own ship.

Making time really is a challenge. This balance dynamic is why we always recommend engaging in activities that are both personally and professionally rewarding. Besides the fact that being genuine is absolutely paramount, doing activities in which you take real pleasure will help to ensure that you participate in them on a regular basis. As an added benefit, it positions you to have something in common with everyone you meet while involved in those activities. These factors will help you develop relationships in more comfortable and meaningful ways.

Avail yourself of the resources not only in this book, but also in your firm and the industry. If you practice in a firm that has marketing and business development and/or practice development professionals, seek them out—they exist to help you and they want to work with you. If that isn't an option for you, invest in a consultant or coach who will assist you in developing and implementing a plan for success. This component of your business is as fundamental as having a telephone or a computer.

WHAT MAKES A SUCCESSFUL RAINMAKER?

Successful rainmakers have different personalities and their practices differ from one another, but they share many of the same qualities. The following attributes (see page 4) that can be ascribed to strong rainmakers remain steadfast through all geographic, practice area, and market condition variables.

As you review the list, consider which of these attributes you think are necessary to be a rainmaker. Perhaps you have other characteristics that come to mind. Our point is that the qualities that many people believe are critical to successful rainmaking are all attributes that can be developed with some assistance and practice, and that you also need them to be a good lawyer.

RAINMAKER ATTRIBUTES[1]

- Good listener
- Strong negotiator
- Confidence
- Curiosity
- Personal contacts
- Persistence
- People skills
- Audacity
- Sense of humor
- Good talker
- Reputation
- Creativity
- Initiative
- Knowledge of industry
- Enthusiastic . . . interested
- Expert in field
- Self-motivated
- Some luck—being in the right place at the right time

Just because you went to a great law school, can draft a terrific memorandum, or know how to solve a legal problem doesn't make you a good lawyer. For example, have you ever been to see a doctor who properly diagnosed you but didn't have a good bedside manner? You probably focused on the doctor's attitude and lack of social skills rather than his medical abilities. Clients evaluate lawyers in exactly the same way.

If you take these attributes and apply them not just to selling but to the way you practice every day, then the people with whom you work will notice. The relationships you establish with clients are critical to success—theirs and yours. Spend a few minutes to take the Great Lawyer Test on the next page.

It is important for all lawyers, but associates in particular, to hone both "soft" and "hard" skill sets. These combined skills are what make lawyers great—from beginning to end of career and from solo practices to the largest, global firms.

[1] As identified by Silvia L. Coulter, CoulterCranston Consulting, Co-Founder, Legal Sales and Service Organization.

THE GREAT LAWYER TEST

- Do you respond to clients within one-half day or less?
- Do your clients know how to reach you in an emergency or after hours?
- Do you know your clients' industries?
- Do you provide value to your clients? How do you know?
- Do you communicate regularly on and off the clock with clients?
- Do you balance the cost of your advice with the potential risk to the client? In other words, do you over-lawyer issues?
- Are you in touch with inactive clients two to three times each year?

MARKETING v. SALES

What's the difference between marketing and sales? It is important to understand the difference and to use the terms correctly.

When clients are considering what lawyers and law firms to hire, there are two primary stages in the process: 1. awareness and 2. rapport and trust. Making potential clients "aware" of you usually happens on a firm level, often called marketing. Developing rapport and gaining trust happen on a personal level; this is often called selling.

Many lawyers use the word "marketing" to refer to all activities involved in generating new business. But corporate America draws a clear distinction between the sales department, which deals directly with clients and revenue generation, and the marketing department that works behind the scenes, deciding which clients to target and how to reach them.

Marketing and sales are two separate and distinct processes, but they are very much intertwined. As we've already implied, marketing exists to support sales. We have included graphics of the marketing cycle (Figure 1) and the stages of personal selling (Figure 2) for you.

The marketing cycle is comprised of four primary sections: market research, planning, visibility, and client development. Personal selling resides in the client development area. The five stages of personal selling are plan, target, and communicate; get to know your market; build relationships; obtain clients; retain clients. While some models of selling processes and client life cycles can be quite complex, we have developed one specifically for associates that is intended to make the roadmap easy to follow.

What words do you think of when you hear the word "SALES?" Take a few seconds now to answer that question. Many lawyers don't associate "SALES" with anything positive. Is it any wonder you may not welcome the thought of selling?!

For many lawyers the idea of selling falls somewhere in the range between undignified and completely abhorrent. Most businesses have sales forces that are entirely separate from the manufacturing and operations people who generate the revenue. In law firms, the same people are responsible for selling and for providing service. So selling is everyone's job in a professional services setting.

Associates should take advantage of that stage of their careers and learn about marketing and selling before the firm expects them to be able to perform those activities well—and before their compensation hinges on it. It isn't smart to wait until you're a partner to start learning these critical skills.

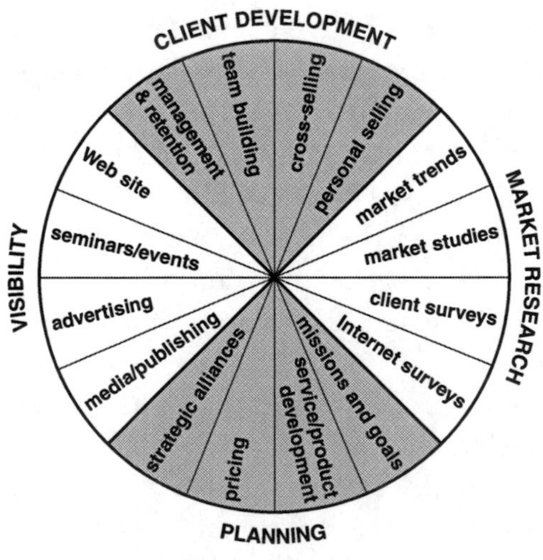

FIGURE 1 The Marketing Process

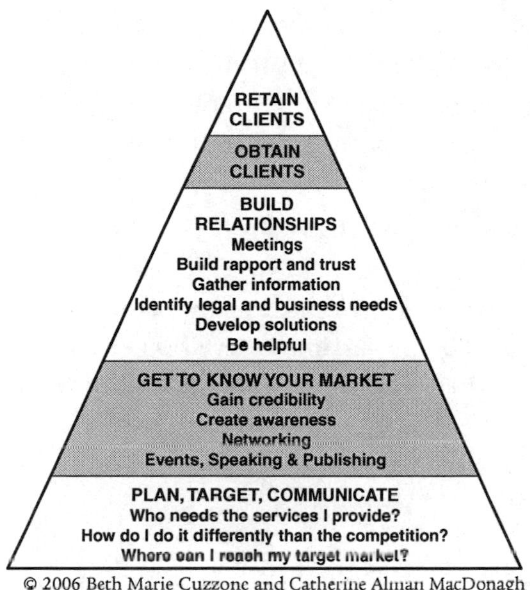

FIGURE 2 The Stages of Personal Selling

Most of us know people we might call "natural rainmakers" (or those who appear gifted). In reality, most top producers in law firms work very hard at developing relationships and the skills required to be successful. So, even if these things happen to already feel natural, you will still benefit from planning, training, coaching, and so forth. Even someone who's an undisputed leader in his field continues to try and improve his game (think Tiger Woods).

For most lawyers, to become adept at marketing and selling takes time and committed effort. It bears repeating: *no one but you can develop and grow your personal relationships.* The best news is that you can learn these skills and you can (and, actually, you must) be yourself.

CHAPTER FLASHBACK

- Providing excellent client service, in its broadest sense, is the key to a successful career.
- Learning how to develop and maintain relationships is at the heart of sales, service, and, ultimately, your success.

- The basic elements of marketing are market research, planning, visibility, and client development.
- The stages of personal selling are plan, target and communicate, get to know your market, build relationships, obtain clients, and retain clients.
- Engage in activities that are both personally and professionally rewarding.
- If you practice in a firm that has marketing and business development and/or professional development professionals, seek them out. They exist to help you, and they want to work with you.

CHAPTER 1

Creating Your Plan

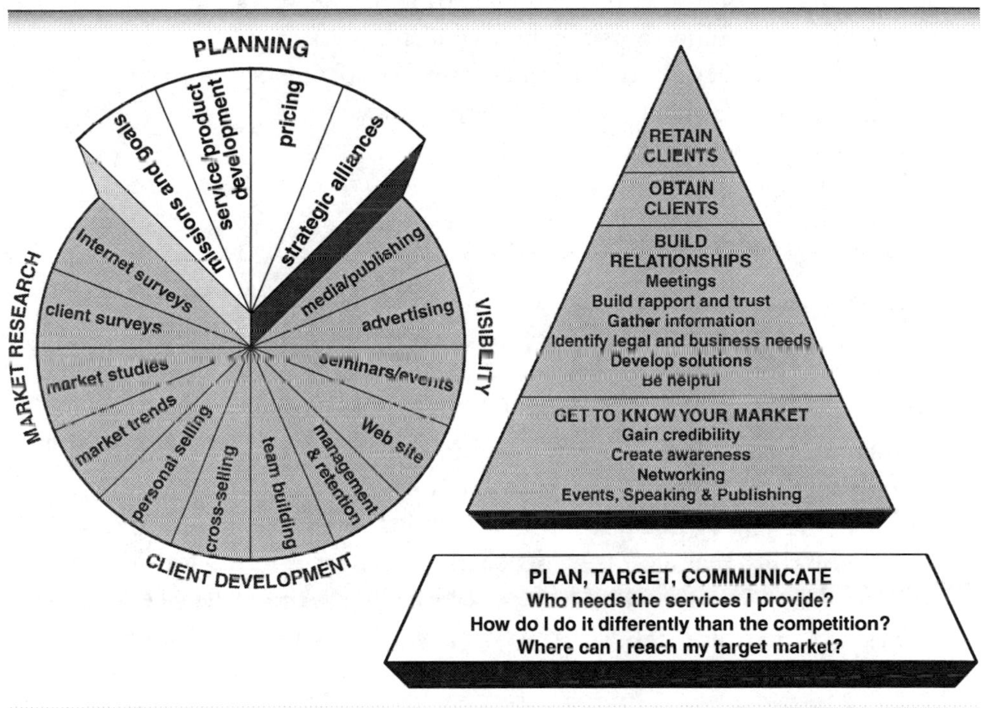

▶ Many associates wrestle with the fact that they are not in control of their own time. Partners, clients, families, friends, community work—there are many things and people that can pull you in many directions, usually all at once. ◀

How do you stay focused and on track so that you are achieving success and continuing to develop your personal marketing and selling skills? The answer: you must have a plan. If you don't know where you're going, any road will get you there. Therefore, we begin with a chapter on creating your plan. If you will follow the steps in this chapter, you will end up with good goals and a solid plan to follow.

There is a reason that this chapter is so lengthy. Each reader has vastly different needs depending on many variables, including years of practice, firm size, resources available, and geographic region. In all situations, the time you take up front to determine who you are, with whom you want to spend your time, where you are going, and how you are going to get there should not be underestimated. We urge you to read this chapter and create a simple plan—not just once, but annually—in which you will determine where to focus and how to spend your marketing and selling time.

IT'S ABOUT YOU

As you begin drafting your plan, remember that it isn't "one size fits all." Also, set yourself up to succeed. That way, you'll be rewarded, you will gain confidence, and you will want to do it again. Don't push yourself too far too fast. Your life and career are marathons, not sprinter's races. Finally, keep in mind that since it's your plan, you are completely free to revise it at any time.

We have provided a form for individual business planning purposes in this chapter. It is comprehensive, but you should feel free to choose the elements that are appropriate for your experience level, practice, firm size, comfort zone, time you are willing to invest, personal and professional interests, and so forth. In other words, consider the form a starting point that you can personalize for your own use.

Once you have planned your activities, lock in deadlines and other important dates on your calendar. When associates are just starting to work with administrative assistants, they sometimes overlook them as a valuable source of support and information. Ask yours to help keep you organized and efficient. Your assistant may also be well-positioned to share suggestions and best practices that specifically apply to you.

THE SMART PLAN

We've all heard the phrase: "plan the work and work the plan." Your individual business plan does not need to be some formal document, since substance is more important than form. However, your plan does need to contain "SMART" goals. SMART is an acronym that stands for *Specific, Measurable, Attainable, Realistic,* and *Timely* (sometimes the *T* stands for "tangible").

Specific: In order to focus your efforts, you must first decide and then very clearly define what it is you are going to do. It sounds simplistic when you first think about it, but it can be difficult to actually do.

Your plan should address what you want to accomplish, what you are going to do, and how you are going to do it. It should also have timelines that indicate your commitment (to yourself) to get it done by a certain date. We all know the power of deadlines.

Measurable: You must measure it so that you can manage it. It is important to set measurable goals and determine concrete ways of evaluating your progress for each one. You will gain a real sense of accomplishment as you make incremental progress. This is as important for staying on track as it is for your confidence and success in maintaining your efforts.

Attainable: When you identify the goals that are most important to you, you begin to figure out ways you can realize them—you develop a vision. You also may begin seeing previously overlooked opportunities.

If you make the mistake of setting goals that you just can't reach, then you won't truly commit to them. The net effect is you will have prevented yourself from being successful. Some lawyers fall into the self-fulfilling prophesy of failure this way. With that said, however, you should definitely reach and stretch yourself.

Realistic: It is important to realize that nothing is going to happen quickly. In addition to the fact that there is a learning curve involved, developing a network and clients takes time and attention. So your annual and mid-term goals must be realistic for you—where you are in your life and your career. Pick goals that you can attain with some effort—aim too high and you set the stage for failure, but aiming too low sends the message that you aren't very ambitious.

Timely: Set a time frame for the goal. Putting an end point on your goal gives you a clear target to work towards. If you don't set a time, the commitment is too vague and invariably, the goal will not be reached. Without a time limit, there's no urgency to start taking action now. The time element must also be measurable, attainable, and realistic.

Example: SMART Goals

Compare the first-stated goal to the SMART goal that follows it and note the differences:

Goal: To have a successful personal injury practice.

SMART Goal: My personal injury practice will reach $250,000 in annual revenue in three years. I will accomplish this by

- furthering relationships with active referral sources, including two insurance agencies and lawyers who do not practice personal injury law;
- keeping in touch with inactive clients three or four times a year (e.g., newsletters, holiday cards, safety and loss prevention updates);
- tracking sources of new business to determine effectiveness of referral, advertising, and other visibility efforts in a contact database; and
- dedicating one hour each week to community visibility (e.g., sponsor local civic activities, especially those related to safety and prevention).

HOW TO IDENTIFY PROSPECTS

Identifying where to start and who to target can be challenging. First, inventory your contacts (see checklist on the next page) and get your database of the people you know into shape. This is a MUST. A good contact list is the cornerstone for most (if not all) marketing and selling efforts.

Capture as much information as you can about your contacts—basic information (addresses, phone numbers, email addresses) is

CONTACTS Defined

▶ Contacts are everyone you know, have ever met, and will meet. Everyone is a prospect, or a client, and/or a referral source!

Family
Friends
Neighbors
Classmates from college, law school, high schools, etc.
Other lawyers
Business people
Community/charitable/religious/other organizations
Acquaintances ◀

critical, of course. But also include where you met the contact or how you know him/her, especially if he/she was introduced to you by someone else—don't rely on your memory. Also, we suggest categorizing your contacts as a prospect, client, or referral source. Some lawyers like to have separate categories for major contact types.

As you will read in Chapters 4 and 5, there are many ways to leverage your marketing successes and to stay in touch with people who are in your network. Investing your time to have a well-organized and maintained contact list will save you time and energy in the future.

Next, use this list to identify prospects. Do this by determining who has direct or indirect influence with people and organizations that are likely to need the legal services you provide. Be overly inclusive to start and recognize that the earlier it is in your career, the more unlikely it is that you will land a "big fish." Remember, your main task is to plant seeds.

A key question at this point is how to define the limits of your search for clients. For example, if you specialize in banking and finance, should you limit your list to organizations that focus on a single specialty, such as syndicated lending, investment banking, or structured finance? Or should your list of potential clients include them all?

This is an important question, and the answer must be determined case by case, depending on a realistic assessment of yourself, your experience, the firm's ability to sell to sub-markets, the resources available for selling, and so forth. It may also be affected by the geography of your competition. In cities like New York and Chicago, where there are many competitors, you may need to focus on a narrower niche. In smaller cities, it may be more practical to aim broadly.

When the time comes to move from strategy to tactics, you must compile a list of the names of people to contact. A firm that chooses investment banking, for example, could start with a list of the organizations that are in its geographic area (since it may be easier to develop relationships with people who are nearby), and then figure out whom to approach in each.

Success in business development demands prioritization, and it is easy to spend too much time with the wrong people. Too often, the people who have the most time for golf and lunch are the people with no need for your services, or have no budget to pay for them.

Therefore, to identify prospects that are worth pursuing, lawyers must narrow down the list to focus their time on the prospects that are most likely to engage the firm within a reasonable period of time. If it does not appear that this is likely, you must move on to the next candidate.

This can be hard to do, because once one has invested time in building a relationship, the natural inclination is to be optimistic that this will lead to new business. This is further complicated by human nature: when you develop a genuine liking for someone, it can be hard to cut back on a business relationship even after it becomes clear that they are not likely to buy. However, keep in mind that this contact may serve as a valuable referral source.

In any event, periodically review and assess your list; prioritization is an important step in any successful campaign. Once it is clear that a person is not going to retain you (or your firm) in the short term nor be helpful to you in building your business, you have a decision to make. Consider demoting that contact from the short list of people who receive your proactive and regular attention, such as valuable "face time," and move it to the longer list of people you can stay in touch with in a more efficient way.

When lawyers first think about selling, many immediately start planning how to find *new* clients. But selling begins at home, and they would have much greater success if they focused first on the clients they already have. Experts agree that, regardless of business or industry, it's much easier to sell to people who know you and have already hired you than to sell to strangers.

You might think that as law firms increase their marketing budgets and hire more business development and marketing professional staff, they would quickly get to the point where their current clients were well taken care of and would no longer be a good source for additional revenue. This seems to be logically inevitable, but it hasn't happened yet. American Lawyer Media's (ALM) 2006 *Law Firm Business Development Practices* survey found that in 2006:

> The largest share of growth by far is from selling more of the same work to existing clients. Selling new work to existing clients and selling work to new clients, each account for much less revenue growth on average.

One way to get started with your current clients is to schedule "off the clock" meetings to learn more about their business needs. At a minimum, this will help build a relationship and protect you from competitors.

In sum, *always* begin with your clients. Active pursuit of new prospects should be left to year two or three of a plan. It's more efficient and a better business investment to make sure that you have penetrated your current client base, are providing as many services as you can to each one, and have created clients who are first satisfied and then loyal before you start spending your time and money on people who don't even know you.

In today's competitive environment, other law firms are working hard to take your best clients, so you will need to put in more effort to protect what you have if you want to keep it.

MEASURING PROGRESS

Obviously, there's a difference between activity and results. To ensure success, you will periodically need to assess whether what you have been trying is working.

Whether you track your activities in a client relationship management (CRM) tool, Outlook, Excel, or on a legal pad, there is one critical thing your "To Do" list must have—a format that you will keep up to date.

Measurements of progress can be subjective or objective. In terms of the former, for example, you might rate your progress about how your relationship with a contact identified in your business plan is progressing, such as whether you've established rapport and built trust. Or you might rate how well you think you understand what is going on in that contact's business or industry. However, objective metrics are also important, as well as somewhat easier to use.

Measurements of Success

- Measuring the conversion rate from the number of meetings you had with people to the number of people who hired you
- Number of meetings with targeted contacts
- Number of new contacts added to your list
- Number of activities to build relationships (remember, it takes an average of six to eight contacts before a prospect becomes a client)
- Billable and billed hours for a particular client
- Fee receipts (all associates should learn basic finance terms like realization rates)
- Originations
- New clients
- New matters
- Proposals and win/partial win rates
- Number of lawyers who participated in client pitches
- Referral rates
- Formal measures of client satisfaction and loyalty
- Percentage of the work in your practice area you have for each client (market share)
- Percentage of the client's total legal budget that is paid to you and your firm (wallet share)

Sample Business Plan

The sample plan that follows is intended to serve as a guide, to stimulate your thinking, and to give you a ready-to-edit form. Not every item in each section will be relevant to you or possible to include.

We stress that the main point of doing a plan is SUBSTANCE, not FORM. It's about the steak, not the sizzle. Over the years, we have seen too much time wasted on creating well-conceived, nice-looking plans that, once finished, only gathered dust on a shelf. Nothing is going to happen if you put all your energy into creating a beautiful plan. The plan is supposed to keep you moving forward. That is why it is so important for your goals to be SMART and for you to take action.

One thing that helps is to keep your plan where you can see it and refer to it when unexpected (but attractive) opportunities arise. This way, your plan stays "top of mind," plus you have a benchmark against which to gauge these opportunities. You can always change your goals, but too often we have seen efforts diverted by the "bright, shiny object" phenomenon that results in a failure to achieve any goal.

We know a lawyer that kept her goals posted right on her computer monitor. This helped her not only to remain focused, but it also allowed her to be flexible enough to seize unforeseen opportunities—if they helped her achieve her goals. Naturally, she was very successful.

Some final pieces of advice before you embark on this planning journey. Build time into your calendar for planning. For example, schedule time at the beginning of each quarter to review your plan. You don't need to take more than 15 minutes to do this. Schedule at least 30 minutes to measure your success at the end of each year. Afterward, make an appointment with yourself at the end of the year. Take at least one hour to create your plan for the following year, allowing enough time to pass so that you have reflected on your progress before doing so.

Start strong. Choose one or two approaches to start with based on what you're best at and what you enjoy doing:

- Networking
- Writing articles
- Blogging

- Public relations
- Speaking
- Teaching

Finally, if you are planning for the first time, keep it simple. Outline a straightforward plan for the next six months. The goal is to maximize the number of people you reach from your target audience. Try it for six months, and then revise the plan. Ask mentors and others you trust and respect for their input.

FORM: INDIVIDUAL BUSINESS PLAN

I. Purpose:

Identify the purpose of this planning document and how it relates to you, your firm, department, and/or practice group objectives.

____

____

____

II. Productivity Goals

Billable Hours ________
Billed Hours ________
Fee Receipts ________
Originations ________
New Clients ________
New Matters ________

How will success be measured?

____

____

____

III. Professional Development

List one to three goals below for your professional development ("short lists," honors, appointments, certifications, specialized training, developing interoffice team for developing and servicing new clients, etc.).

Describe any legal education that you feel is needed to increase your expertise in the areas in which you now practice or would like to practice in the future.

IV. Business Development (Sales)

A. Prior Year's Business Development

1. Describe how you obtained additional business from existing clients this year. Identify significant clients and the types of work generated.

2. Describe significant marketing activities you participated in (speaking and writing, trade, professional, and business organizations, and seminars).

3. List your most notable cases or transactions last year with marketing or client development significance.

4. Evaluate your business development strengths and weaknesses for you or the firm to address.

B. Cross-selling / Teamwork

1. How successful/not successful were you in introducing your clients to other lawyers and what changes do you plan to make in the coming year (list clients and lawyers)?

____

____

____

2. How were you successful/not successful in distributing work to (or receiving work from) other lawyers or practice groups? What changes do you plan to make in the coming year? List the types of work and lawyers:

____

____

____

C. This Year's Marketing and Business Development Plan

1. Goals

What do you want to accomplish? List up to three goals for your business and client development efforts in the coming year and beyond.

____

____

____

2. Client Development Opportunities

List the largest and/or best clients (5–10+) you have now/used to work for that have potential for additional business and/or cross-selling other firm services.

____

____

____

____

____

____

3. New Clients (Prospects) and Referral Sources

List your top prospects (5–10+) and referral sources you will be developing and continuing relationships with this year.

____
____
____
____
____
____

4. Cross-selling

(Cross-selling, in its simplest terms, is servicing the same client across different practice areas.)

Identify the services either currently offered or needed by the firm that you think are important to your selling efforts.

____
____
____

Where are the best opportunities for cross-selling?

____
____
____

5. Activities

Memberships

____
____
____

Speaking

____
____
____

Publishing

____

____

____

Firm-sponsored seminars/workshops/events

____

____

____

Community organizations

____

____

____

Pro bono work

____

____

____

6. How will progress be measured?

____

____

____

CHAPTER FLASHBACK

- You must have a plan and you should put it in writing. Create one annually to determine where you will focus and how to spend your marketing and selling time.
- Set "SMART" goals.
- Keep your contact list current. It is the cornerstone of your marketing and business development activities.
- Focus on expanding relationships with existing clients first and always.

- Schedule "off the clock" meetings to learn more about clients' business needs.
- Make your "To Do" list in a format that you will keep up to date.
- Each December, schedule 15 minutes on your calendar at the beginning of each quarter to review your plan. Schedule at least 30 minutes to measure your success at the end of each year. Afterward, schedule a follow-up time for at least one hour to create your plan for next year, allowing time to reflect on your progress before doing so.

CHAPTER 2

Communicating Your Plan

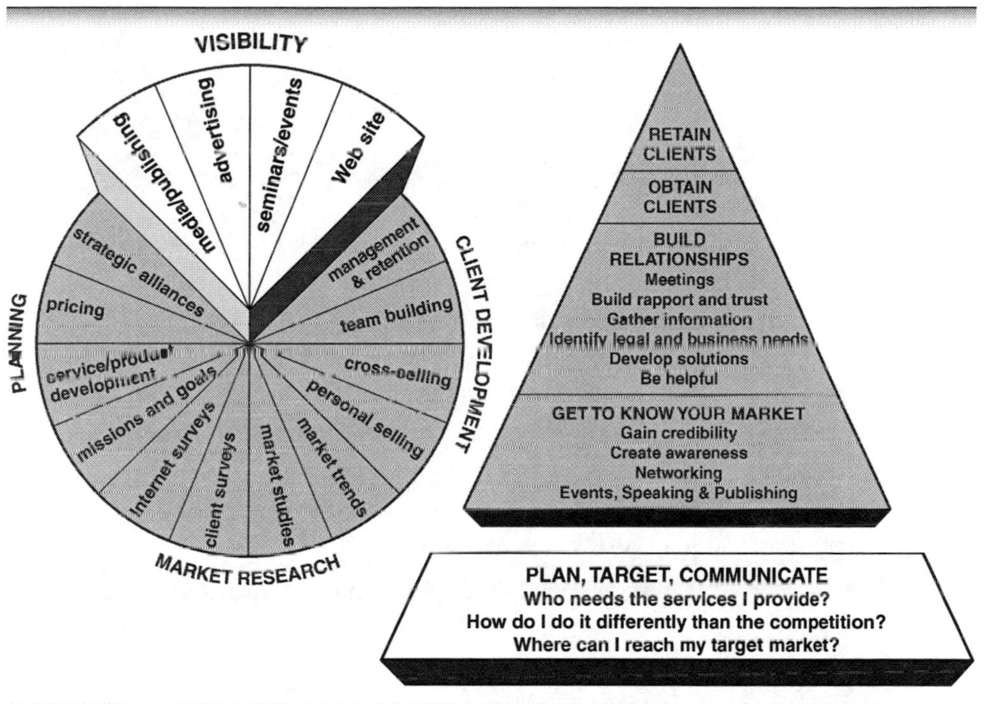

► Now that you have created a plan that identifies your goals and the actions you will take to achieve them, you must communicate this plan. This means taking action in the areas identified as "Visibility" in the Marketing Process diagram. ◄

Everything speaks. Your business cards, Web site, print materials, dress code, and professional photo all help to communicate your unique position, brand, image, values, and reputation to the market. Your brand is what you promise to the marketplace. The market is clients, prospects, referral sources, the community at large, and, for most associates, partners. As we remind you throughout this book, consider everyone, including all the personnel in your firm, to be your "sales force." Since you never know who knows whom, someone you least expect could be a potential referrer.

This chapter provides you with principles and guidelines to consider when creating the marketing and communication pieces that support you and help you achieve your goals.

YOUR BIOGRAPHY

Your bio is probably the marketing tool you will use most frequently, so it is worth spending time to create one that will be effective. For starters, it will be used as a stand-alone piece or in combination with your printed materials. It will also be posted on your Web site. More business is coming in via Internet searches than ever before, and many visitors go right to biographies–and make the decision to keep reading or not within the first few sentences. Obviously, you want them to keep reading.

You may also use your bio when you

- meet, work with, or follow up with a client, prospect, or referral source;
- speak;
- publish;
- submit for awards and recognition; and
- appear before a judge who is unfamiliar with you.

There are four key focus areas: your introductory paragraph, search engines, representative experience, as well as regular updates. The following are some tips about each and how to maximize your biography's performance:

1. Your Introductory Paragraph

This is the narrative section of your biography. It is also the first place searched by search engines. It should be easy to read, impressive, and helpful:

- *Observe the "no scroll rule."* Keep your most current and relevant experience at the top. When your bio is used online, this keeps the reader from having to scroll down.
- *No legalese*–you want to convey to the reader that you can and will speak the language of their business, not the language of law.
- *Brevity is key.* Touch briefly on your main practice focus(es) and then expand on your areas of concentration if they aren't listed as practice area pages on the Web site.
- *List honors and other recognition* you've received.

2. Search Engines

Most people find lawyers online in this way: they type a search string (into Google®, Yahoo!®, etc.) such as "employment" "lawyers" "Boston." So, in order to improve search engine visibility:

- *Use specific industry terms.* Think like a potential client. What would she search for?
- *Use the words "law," "lawyer," "lawyer,"* and as many names of *cities and states* as you can. Mention the office(s) and cities in which you work and list all states in which you are admitted to practice. Remember, the point is to direct as many people as you can to your site via the search engines.
- Any items related to diversity/inclusion should be integrated. These have proven to be a hot search trend.

3. Representative Experience List

This could be the most important item on your bio, since many readers go straight to it. As a general rule, associates should have five to ten items on their representative matters list. If your introduction is the appetizer, your representative matters list is the main course. Therefore, it should

- be up-to-date,
- show a range of experience,
- contain very specific industry terms, and
- be compliant with your state bar rules of advertising.

4. Update Regularly

Review your introductory paragraph, representative matters, and your photo periodically. Make sure they are kept current.

PROFESSIONAL PHOTOGRAPH: A MUST

Regardless of your personal preference, a professionally-done photo is a must for your Web and marketing materials. Keep in mind that people buy from people they know and like and that a photo will facilitate the impression of familiarity. It humanizes an otherwise impersonal medium. This is why photos are used in marketing across industry lines.

TIPS FOR A GREAT PHOTO

- Get your hair cut two to three weeks before your photo.
- No floral or busy print patterns—solid colors are best.
- Navy is always a safe choice for lawyers.
- Avoid large jewelry that will distract.
- Stay away from trendy looks.
- No high-necked blouses/turtlenecks.
- Relax your face.
- It is OK to SMILE! You want to appear serious, competent, *and* approachable.
- Men with heavy beards should make morning appointments. ◀

YOUR WEB SITE AND WRITTEN MATERIALS (AND HOW TO USE THEM)

Your materials represent you and leave a lasting impression, so it is important to think about how you want to appear to your target market. If you want to convey substance and professionalism, then don't have cheap, sloppy looking collateral. Remember that everything speaks—the design, the colors, the paper choice, the font (please, don't use comic sans), and the overall appearance. They are an extension of your brand.

Your written materials include an overview of you, your firm and practice, your differentiators, your culture, your service model, and your commitment to clients. Include professional-looking brochures, article reprints, materials related to recent presentations, lists of representative clients/matters, and your biography. You may also include things like your fee schedule, if appropriate.

Many times, lawyers struggle with how to follow up with a prospect or what is the next step in developing a relationship. Usually, that is because they haven't given themselves the opportunity for continuing a dialogue. Developing materials that demonstrate you have listened to what the prospect has told you, especially if the materials are helpful to them, will advance a relationship.

Many firms have used Web sites and blogs as great marketing tools and lead generators. Web sites are a must now. Design them for different purposes for best results: for prospective clients to perform the due diligence aspect of the "screening" phase of buying and for clients to whom you want to deliver stellar service and "added value." Consider including a feature that allows visitors to subscribe to a complimentary newsletter in subject areas by industry or business type.

Do NOT bring canned materials to a meeting. This mistake allows you no opportunity to reflect back to your prospect that you have any understanding of their needs or issues. It also has a tendency to appear arrogant; in effect, you are telling your prospective client or referral source that you already know what they need rather than that you are interested in identifying those needs, listening to them, and building a relationship.

Written materials do not sell—YOU do. Written materials inform, and good ones can give a prospect a snapshot of what it's like to do business with you. They must be used as an aid or tool to build a relationship. This means don't compete with your materials and don't use them as a crutch. They should support your conversations and be used as a follow-up to—rather than as an introduction at your meetings. Therefore, your materials should be in a flexible format so that you can respond and follow up with specific, on-point information.

Use the communications checklist below to help you decide where to focus.

CHECKLIST: Communications

- Write a bio that gets read.
- Have nice-looking materials.
- Reread the "who" section of your marketing plan, and remind yourself to choose tactics that increase visibility to the audience you have selected.
- In articles, speeches and ads, create a call to action in the substance of each. Give the market a reason to contact you. Checklists, "takeaways," strategies, or bullet points of advice work well. Make sure they contain your contact information.
- If you are going to advertise, you must run ads frequently. We do not recommend one or two ads. Repetition is KEY.
- In your advertising, comply with your state bar rules, and be sure your message is larger then your name. Include your phone number, email, and Web site addresses.
- If you have a Web site, include a "contact" button that allows someone to contact you via email. Check the *Lawyer's Guide to Marketing on the Internet*, Third Edition by Gregory H. Siskind, Deborah McMurray and Richard P. Klau.
- Utilize the back of your business card. Suggestions: mission statement, list of practice areas, or your differentiator (for example, you are focused on intellectual property and have a science degree).
- Don't just speak anywhere. Giving excellent presentations is time-consuming, so identify the opportunities that help you reach your intended audience. Also, "repurpose" materials.

SPEAKING THAT GETS RESULTS

Public speaking is an important aspect of a marketing or communications plan for any law firm. Speaking at the right conferences and seminars offered by your firm, organizations, association, and industry trade groups increases your visibility and enhances your credibility. You will also be able to meet prospects and referral sources and develop deeper relationships with existing clients and referral sources. Being a speaker often is more comfortable for lawyers in connecting with attendees because they are in the "faculty" category.

Don't just speak anywhere. Giving excellent presentations is time-consuming, so identify the speaking opportunities that help you reach your intended audience. Also, "repurpose" your materials. For example, turn your presentation into an article (or vice versa)—it will help build visibility if you are consistent in your approach.

When you speak, create ways for people to connect with you—and for you to connect with them. Have a theme. Tell a good story. Be personable. Have a call to action. Be aware of the different learning styles and personality types (covered in Chapter 6) and make sure your presentation has something for each. Practice your presentation and become facile with visual aids, such as PowerPoint and flip charts, so that you are using them as the supporting tools they were intended to be, rather than as a replacement to the main attraction—you. Have fun! If you are enjoying yourself and are relaxed, the audience will be too.

Always give your attendees a reason to contact you after the program, and include your phone number and email address on everything, even program evaluations. You never know what attendees will take with them. During your lectures and speeches, provide attendees with a form to fill out if they would like you to contact them, add them to your mailing or email list, or even meet with them in the near future. Reference an article, template, or checklist in your program and then invite the audience to leave a business card so that you can send it to them. After the program, add all new contacts to your database, update contacts with any new information, and follow up. Where appropriate, use branded, giveaway items like pens or note pads that have contact information on them.

All lawyers should seek and receive training for public speaking as they are expected to be able to present well in front of clients and the general population. Consider registering for a program such as the "*Public Speaking for Lawyers*" course offered by ALI-ABA (American Law Institute–American Bar Association). This particular program qualifies for mandatory CLE credit in certain states, a terrific way to get two important things taken care of at one time.

Here's an overview of that program's published highlights:

Preparation

- *The audience:* The importance of getting information about its size, needs, demographics, and familiarity with your subject
- *Selecting a topic:* How to tailor your topic to fit the audience, the occasion, and your objectives
- *Publicity:* How provocative titles stimulate interest and attendance; how to be newsworthy and quotable–and get maximum mileage by using press releases, advance copies, and reprints
- *Arrangements:* How to use seating configurations and lighting to your advantage
- *Introductions:* What is said before you come to bat is too important to be left to chance; how to take control and write your own introductions; how to recover from a poor introduction

The Speech

- *Gathering information:* Using reference books, statistical materials, quotations, and expert opinions to make your speech authoritative and informative
- *Language:* Developing a simple, direct style that scores
- *Humor:* When and how to use it; when it should be avoided

Delivery

- *Conquering fear:* How the pros do it
- *Creating an image:* Appearance, mental and physical preparation, nonverbal communication

- *Developing a good speaking voice:* Timing techniques; using pacing, pitch, and volume to add variety and rivet audience attention
- *Notes:* How and when to use them, memory devices, reading effectively
- *Using a microphone:* Successful microphone techniques, coping with public-address systems, using long cords and wireless microphones
- *Handling question and answer sessions:* Grace under fire

Finally, you might consider working with an executive presentation coach when you have a really important speech to make. Your remarks need not be long for you to make an impact; we recall some memorable speakers whose only task was to introduce someone else. Another resource is Toastmasters International, which is a group (with chapters in most cities) that meets regularly to work on speaking skills.

CHECKLIST: When You're Presenting

- Prepare so that you feel confident—and rehearse!
- Run on time.
- Have a timed agenda or outline.
- Tell them what:
  - You are going to show them
  - You are showing them
  - You just showed them.
- Show + Tell = Sell.
- Be aware of different learning styles and have something in your program for all of them.
- Use the power of your voice, gestures, pauses, and eye contact to connect with your audience.
- Be genuine and professional, engaging, and memorable.
- Embed memorable messages with compelling stories into your presentation.

- Use visual aids masterfully.
- Give something away.
- Create ways to connect–and follow up.
- Follow up, follow up, follow up.

CHAPTER FLASHBACK

- Everything speaks.
- Many Web site visitors go right to biographies–and make the decision to keep reading or not within the first few sentences.
- Your introductory paragraph is the narrative section of your biography, and it is also the first place searched by search engines.
- Use specific industry terms. Think like a potential client.
- A professionally-done photograph is a must. People buy from people they know and like.
- Your written materials should include an overview of you, your firm and practice, your differentiators, your culture, your service model, and your commitment to clients.
- Do not bring materials to any meeting unless specifically requested to do so.
- Written materials do not sell–YOU do. They must be used as an aid or tool to build a relationship.
- Identify the speaking opportunities that help you reach your intended audience(s).
- "Repurpose" your materials and leverage your investment of time.
- During your lectures and speeches, provide attendees with a form to fill out if they would like you to contact them or meet with them in the near future. Try inviting your audience to leave a business card if they'd like you to send them an article or other helpful follow-up.
- Add new names to your contact list. Ask people who call where they found out about you and capture that information to see what activities are resulting in visibility.

CHAPTER 3

Getting to Know Your Target Market— The Power of a Network

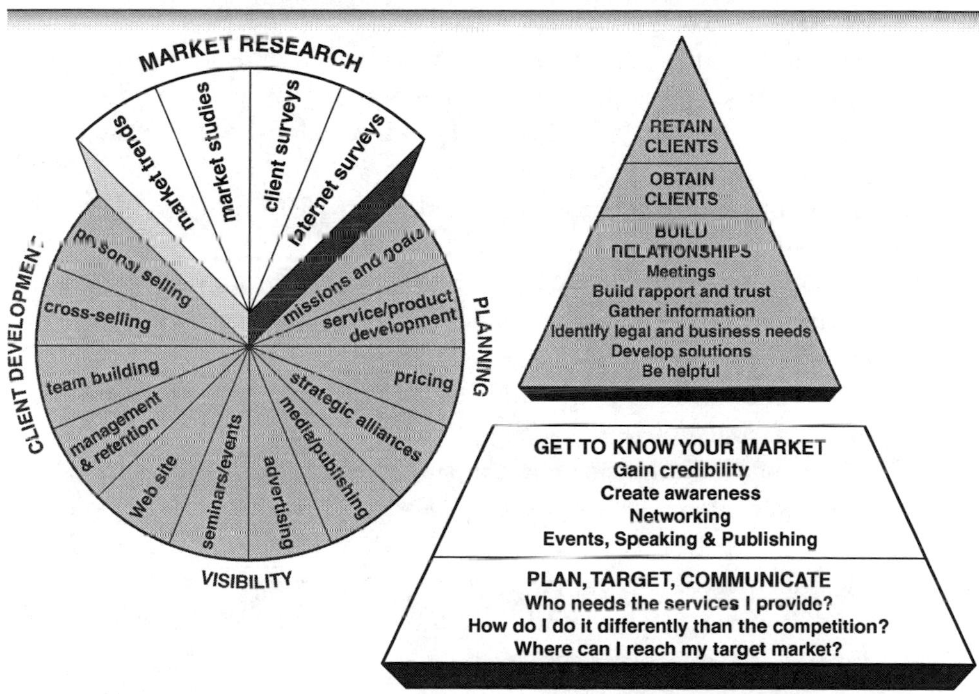

PEOPLE ARE YOUR GREATEST RESOURCES

▶ If you want to be successful, you must add networking to your skill set and continually improve this ability. The more you understand

about the power of networks and the different kinds of relationships that will help you at each stage of your marketing and sales processes, the more empowered and successful you will become. ◄

Sure, networking is connecting with and meeting people with whom you will do business. But it is also about helping others–you must give to get.

It is well established that people prefer to do business with others whom they know, like, and trust. Networking should expand the number of people who know, like, and trust you. The ability to establish trust and rapport quickly is a foundational skill that you can and must learn. It is the single most important requirement in building a relationship.

To network more effectively, listen more than you talk in any conversation. When you meet someone new, spend most of your time asking that person questions about herself and her business. This positions you to ask the person to describe what's going on and what she cares about. Ask how you might be helpful to her. Who is her ideal customer? Do you know anyone who fits her description? You do not need to talk about yourself in order to find out about something she needs in her life and business.

Associates, especially early in their careers, are uniquely positioned to ask business leaders for advice, secrets to their success and their opinions on what makes a great lawyer, and what they should do with their careers. The business leaders may suggest joining industry associations or reading certain publications. You should embrace mentors wherever you can find them in the business community. In the process, you develop relationships that may become the pillars of your network.

In short, you need a network. Give to others and help them. If you do this in an efficient and organized fashion, what you give will come back to you many times over.

DEVELOPING, CULTIVATING, AND MAINTAINING A NETWORK

While many approach networking with the same degree of enthusiasm as getting the tartar scraped off their teeth, it is a critical part of the process and you should master it.

Where can you network? In short, everywhere! The place that many associates think of first is bar association events. These can be important for everyone and are crucial for those who need to develop a referral network with colleagues. It's also a great starting point for associates, since it's relatively safe and they have something in common with everyone there. This helps build confidence.

We always encourage lawyers to attend industry/trade association events. Associates have great opportunities to "get in at the ground floor" here. That is because everyone understands that you as an associate are just starting out. No one expects you to know their business yet, so it's the perfect time to meet people and ask about their business issues. Gaining an understanding of them now allows you to better sell solutions later. If you already belong to associations, you must be engaged. Attend meetings regularly and get involved in committees that offer you good visibility and good opportunities for developing relationships with your targets.

Other valuable resources for lawyers in firms of any size that are often overlooked are ancillary service providers that are targeting the same market. Teaming up with them is usually a good idea (and can be an especially effective strategy for solo practitioners), since it allows you to be efficient with your time and resources. You can simultaneously develop a relationship with your referral sources as well as conduct targeted efforts to the market you want to reach.

Besides maximizing your time, marketing and selling with others will help to expand your comfort zone. If you and a similarly situated accountant, for example, attend a networking event together, you can tag team and help each other with introductions, conversations, and exits.

In addition to connecting with and learning from other people, there is a wealth of online resources to tap. Join mailing lists and list serves on the Web; read blogs to see what people are saying. These are readily available tools that help you to learn more about (and stay abreast of) the industry needs within a target market.

Also, you can use news-clipping services to stay current on issues, legislation, people, and companies. The additional benefits of networking are that it helps you find reasons to connect with people as well as anticipate things that will affect your clients and prospects. Nothing is more helpful or says "I am thinking about you and your business" more than a proactive outreach that includes a solution.

If you are an associate who is not in direct contact with clients, giving helpful information is appreciated and remembered by partners as well. It's a great way for associates to "add value." Work with law librarians or suppliers of information products and ask them to help you. For lawyers in firms without this resource, seek out your local social law librarian. The business information you find can also be relevant to the legal work you are doing in some unexpected ways. Please do not assume that the partner for whom you are working, even if she is a superstar in client development, has the same information, questions, or ideas you do about a particular client.

We also like the idea of attending other firms' seminars. Many times, the presenting firm will not have their lawyers in the audience. This leaves the opportunities for engaging their attendees to their competitors.

A rather elementary but often forgotten tactic: carry your business cards with you at all times—you never know whom you will meet or where you will meet him or her.

TIPS

CONVERSATION STARTERS AND EFFECTIVE NETWORKING QUESTIONS

- How did you get into your industry?
- How have you grown your business over the last couple years?
- What is your company's vision? And what is it doing to achieve it?
- Who are your main competitors?
- Are there any legal, regulatory, or market uncertainties affecting your business, or changes of any sort that particularly concern you?
- How do you work with outside counsel?
- Is there anything that dissatisfies you about the level of legal services you've been getting?
- What criteria do you use in selecting lawyers? What do you think makes a good lawyer? ◀

TIPS **NETWORKING—BEFORE THE RECEPTION/EVENT**

- Attend with an objective or goal in mind—set one attainable, realistic goal for the event and write it down (e.g., meet two individuals and collect two business cards).
- Get and review a copy of the attendee list in advance.
- Think about who will be attending. Whom do you want to meet? Who can you introduce to whom?
- Pick at least one name from the registration list to call. "I noticed you were also attending the conference—are you going to the reception as well? I would like to take a few minutes and visit with you about your industry/company."
- Review your elevator pitch (see page 45) and revise it to include something related to the event. Practice. Look in the mirror and practice while smiling (but avoid looking like the Cheshire cat). ◀

Exit Strategies

We've all been there—attached to someone, seemingly for the evening, when we KNOW we have to meet others at a networking event. Since this aspect of networking seems to cause a good deal of anxiety (it's right up there with attending an event solo where you don't think you'll know anyone), we've given it its own section.

Here are exit strategies that allow you to leave gracefully and move on to making the next contact:

1. Spend no more than four to nine minutes with any one individual.
2. Keep one hand free to shake hands—meaning eat or drink, but don't do both.
3. Make a plan to follow up.
4. Introduce contacts to each other.
5. Reinforce the follow-up.
6. Don't make it obvious that you want to move on to meeting the next person.
7. Close the conversation well.

TIPS NETWORKING—AT THE RECEPTION/EVENT

- Think of yourself more as a host as opposed to a guest, even if you are not the host or even a sponsor of the event. Just as you would be warm and welcoming and introduce guests to one another if they were in your home, do so at a business event.
- Arrive early if it is you/your firm hosting the event.
- Always wear your nametag on the right—this keeps your name in the other person's line of vision when you shake hands (many people are visual learners—see section on Learning Styles in Chapter 6).
- Focus on introductions and relationships, not selling.
- If you notice someone uncomfortable due to another's behavior, gently insert yourself into the interaction and help the person get out of the conversation.
- Never sit at an empty table or next to an empty chair.
- If you're attending with colleagues, DON'T CLUMP TOGETHER. Divide and conquer!
- Introduce new contacts to one another.
- Position yourself near the door, bar, or food table where there is more traffic.
- Avoid spending a lot of time with people you already know (unless they have an opportunity to give you a cross-introduction).
- Look for individuals in the room with "white knuckles." Although they may be wallflowers, they might be valuable to spend time with and they'll appreciate your gesture.
- Go for quality, meaningful connections.
- Bring business cards. Even though this is on the list, it is more important to get business cards; make notes right then and there about how to follow up (that means you need to bring a pen too).
- Be prepared to give, not get; i.e., be helpful.
- If you forget someone's name, either try just admitting it ("I'm sorry, but I've forgotten your name!") or introduce that person to someone you know ("Oh, have you met Kenna?") and then wait for the two people to introduce themselves to each other.
- Watch your body language: maintain eye contact and keep your distance—an arm's length. ◀

TIPS **EFFECTIVE CONVERSATIONS**

- Spend most of your time asking questions about others.
- Observe the 80/20 Rule: Listen attentively at least 80 percent of the time and speak 20 percent or less of the time.
- Pause before speaking.
- Repeat what you hear during the course of a conversation—it reflects that you're listening and it clarifies points.
- Refer back to points of information shared earlier in the dialogue. "As you said earlier. . . ."
- Try to find two things in common with the other person.
- Focus on being interested versus interesting ("Enough about me, let's talk about ME!").
- Don't offer your card until you have made a connection with the other person or established some kind of rapport. ◀

TIPS **BUSINESS CARDS**

- It is important both to receive and give business cards. But start by asking for one, not offering yours, and then spend time examining the card.
- Later, make notes on the back of a person's business card about your conversations and your follow-up action items with good contacts.
- Keep your business cards in an easy to reach pocket or purse. Don't dig. Also be sure to keep the cards you collect from others in a separate pocket or place so that you don't end up giving out someone else's card instead of your own.
- Write something related to your conversation on your card—when the contact returns to her office, she is more likely to look at the card that has handwriting on it than other cards in her stack from the event. ◀

TIPS AFTER THE RECEPTION/EVENT

- Follow up as soon as possible with everyone.
- If you have offered to send someone information, set up a meeting, etc., do it within three business days.
- Send thank-you notes. A handwritten note is far more powerful than an email.
- Review the cards you collected and the attendee list to form a follow-up plan for each person with whom you want to further a relationship. Find something to ask him or her to send you.
- Capture in your contact database/CRM:
  - all information related to new contacts, including a reference as to where you met;
  - all new information related to existing contacts you may have learned at the event;
  - specific information that will impress your contact if you can recall it later (names of children, for example);
  - your activities;
  - any follow-up plans (this will help you both stay organized and actually follow up); and
  - the contact's "category" (e.g., "small business owner") so that you can easily and efficiently run targeted marketing and sales lists (e.g., mailings or call lists). ◄

CLOSING CONVERSATIONS

There are many ways to finish a conversation and move on to the next one. It's perfectly fine to say that you have to make a phone call, get a drink, go to the restroom, or say hello to someone else.

Here are some other ideas to try:

- Say, "Excuse me, I see someone I need to say hello to."
- Don't be afraid to say, "I don't want to monopolize your time; although I've enjoyed talking to you, I know there are other people we both need to speak to."

- Say, "It's been great talking with you. Good luck with that project you're working on."
- Use nonverbal cues such as extending your hand, stepping aside from the conversation circle, and putting down your drinking glass.
- Say, "I've enjoyed meeting you. Have a great evening."
- Say, "Thank you, you've been interesting to talk to, I'm going to go meet some more people."
- Shake hands and look him/her in the eye: "I appreciate your talking with me and now I'm going to talk to others with whom I need to speak before the event ends/meeting begins."
- Say, "I'm so glad we met tonight. It would be great if I could take your card so that when I meet others who would be interested in you/your service/your product, I could refer them to you."
- Ask, "May I have your card?"
- Say, "It was really great meeting you tonight; I look forward to following up with you about _____."

LISTENING IS KEY

If you're not talking, you're not selling. One of the most important skills you MUST develop is listening.

In *The Seven Habits of Highly Effective People* (Free Press, Rev. Ed., 2004), Stephen Covey wrote: "If I were to summarize the single most important principle in the field of interpersonal relationships, listening is the key." A qualitative research study showed that one of the best metrics for tracking success is whether rainmakers consistently listen to their clients.[1]

Why is listening so hard for many lawyers? Well, first of all, you must talk less. But if you want selling to be easier, engage in active, sincere listening. The more you listen, the more fascinating the

[1] "Increasing Marketing Effectiveness at Professional Firms," a survey published by Suzanne Lowe and Larry Bodine in 2006.

other person will find you! Too often, we interrupt to finish someone's sentence, are already formulating a response, or make it obvious that we are only waiting for the right time in the conversation to make our point. Stop doing those things.

Experts say that when you are building business relationships, you should spend 50 to 80 percent of your time listening. But when lawyers meet potential clients, so many seem to think that they need to talk—and do it quickly—so they can list all the wonderful things that they and their firm can do. Who wants to be in that kind of a relationship with a lawyer? No one!

People are more interested in their own problems than in your capabilities. So apply this understanding and devote most of your time to focusing on what each person wants, needs, and feels.

Great listeners also don't argue. That's another reason many lawyers find it difficult. To listen effectively, you must give up the need to be right.

There are dozens of books to read, and even a professional academic organization you can join (the International Learning Association, www.listen.org). Meanwhile, these five steps can get you started:

1. Establish genuine interest by asking questions and carefully listening to the answers.
2. Take notes. Writing down what people say shows that what they say is important, and that you are paying attention.
3. Respond to the speaker's nonverbal cues, and monitor your own (see the sections in Chapter 6 on Learning Styles and Personality Types).
4. Paraphrase, summarize, and restate what you hear. When you reflect back what people say, they will think that you are smart and likable—especially if you don't disagree, interrupt, or argue.
5. Be prepared with good questions.

Lawyers should ask questions that will help a client think through a situation without trying to push her to a particular conclusion or distracting her.

For example, try a variation on the "5 Whys" approach used in process improvement. For any situation, ask "Why?" at least five times to get to the crux of the matter. If you keep asking "why" to get to the real need, you won't have to work so hard at developing a solution and "closing" the business won't be so difficult either.

Keep asking questions that draw out information, layer by layer, until the client and the lawyer are satisfied that all the important points have been covered, such as

- Tell me more about ____.
- Give me an example of ____.
- What else should I know about ____?

This approach also allows you to obtain access to other topics without forcefully changing the subject. These non-threatening questions introduce a new topic, but still leave the client free to take the conversation wherever she wants. For example:

- How does ____ fit the picture?
- Talk to me about your experience with ____.
- How do you handle ____?

It sounds simple, but asking these types of question does not come naturally to many lawyers because they like to be in control. Well, clients do too. Professional sales people have a saying that "whoever talks the most will enjoy the meeting the most." If you want to build and maintain your relationships, you want the prospect or client to be the one who enjoys the meeting.

YOUR INTRODUCTORY DESCRIPTION—A.K.A. THE "ELEVATOR PITCH"

Your "elevator pitch" is your introduction and description of who you are and what you do. It is your opportunity to define (or redefine) your personal brand or your reputation. Communicating your elevator pitch to others allows them to remember how you help people. An added benefit is that other people can literally be your commercial.

Below are guidelines and a short exercise to assist you in creating your self-introduction.

What it is:

- 10–20 seconds in duration
- A sound bite
- Succinct and memorable
- Spotlights your uniqueness
- Focused on benefits
- Delivered effortlessly

Rules for an Effective Elevator Pitch:

- It must pass the "so what?" test
- Do not say, "I'm a partner/counsel/associate/solo"
- No sales pitch
- No legal-ease!
- Try this: "My name is __________, and I help ___________."

Guidelines:

- Keep it short.
- Think "tagline."
- Solve a problem.
- Point out the benefits.
- Be excited about your work!
- Be genuine.
- Practice makes perfect.
- Use the elevator pitch worksheet to get started.

Example: My name is Kenna. Kenna O'Donnell. I help commercial real estate developers with their contracts in major cities all over the world.

TIP ► Repeating your first name as in the example above helps people remember it. ◄

FORM: ELEVATOR PITCH WORKSHEET

What are your deliverables? Identify services or features.

____

____

____

____

Write a list of benefits your clients derive from working with you (make sure they pass the "so what?" test).

____

____

____

____

Combine the deliverables with the benefits to write your 15–25-second elevator pitch. PRACTICE IT (try looking in the mirror too—body language is important!) until you can say it effortlessly.

____

____

____

____

TIP

► Many lawyers provide more than one legal service to more than one group of professionals. Remember to tailor your elevator pitch to the person with whom you are speaking or the situation in which you are networking. For example, if you are a business lawyer, you will introduce yourself differently to a start-up entrepreneur than an in-house lawyer at a multinational company. If you have no information about the person, try using the event itself as a way to establish a connection. ◄

HOW TO KEEP IN TOUCH WITH YOUR NETWORK

As an associate, keep in mind that some of the contacts, counterparts, and colleagues you know today will grow into positions with either the authority to hire lawyers or the ability to influence a hiring decision in the future. Career progression, like developing relationships, is a long-term process. You must keep in touch with your contacts over time in order for them to think of you when the time is right.

In other words, don't wait until your classmate is appointed General Counsel to reach out to her for the first time in years when you want her to do something for you. It's not likely to be well received. At this point, you might be viewed more as an intrusion than an asset.

With all that in mind, one of the most important things you can do is to maintain and keep in touch with prospects, clients, and referral sources.

It takes *an average* of six to eight contacts with a prospect before closing the business. Don't stop communications if you are not hired during the first few interactions. Here are a few ways to insure you keep in touch with your prospect:

1. After meeting a new business colleague, enter their contact and all relevant information into your database.
2. Touch base with all individuals in your database at least four times a year.
3. Always follow up in a timely manner.
4. Send articles written by lawyers in different practice areas to prospects.
5. If you don't win the business from a Request for Proposal (also known as an RFP or pitch), be sure to stay in contact with the decision-maker. "Number two" is a good place to be in the event of a conflict situation or when the decision-maker isn't satisfied with the current lawyer.
6. When you buy a table at an event, fill it with a mix of clients and prospects and the right lawyers from your firm.
7. Always send a follow-up correspondence after a meeting with a referral source or prospect.

Of course, you are in the best position to help yourself when you're already in front of a prospect, client, or referrer. Before you conclude your conversation, make sure you have what's called in billiards "a good leave" so that you've already built in your follow-up action(s). In sales talk, it's called the *advance*.

In 2003, Mark Maraia wrote and published *Rainmaking Made Simple*, which stated an advance has three elements: (1) a commitment (2) to take action (3) in a definite time period. For complex legal matters, the advance often involves getting a meeting with others who may be involved in making the decision to buy.

TIPS **HOW TO MAINTAIN CONTACT**

- Capture what you know about a client or prospect in a database. Use ticklers to remember important dates, such as birthdays and anniversaries (with the firm/company).
- Use your contact database or CRM system (or paper trail) to capture notes from your conversations with referral sources and prospects.
- Use newsletters, alerts, and updates to give just enough information to pique interest and give contacts a reason to remember and call you. If you categorize your contacts while you are entering them into (or updating) your database, you will be able to send specific mailers to targeted groups easily and efficiently.
- Allow space in your newsletters for clients to showcase their accomplishments such as promotions, awards, announcements, and seminars.
- If you don't have time to talk or if you simply want a short "keep-in-touch" call, try this before- or after-hours tip to save time and improve your chances of getting voicemail: Leave a message saying that you were thinking of him/her and called to say a quick hello. ◀

Sometimes, lawyers get to a point where they feel like they have been setting up good meetings but they're not getting anywhere. If that happens to you, this simple strategy of how to prepare for every business development meeting might help. First, write down what you think the person's needs will be, any objections the person will have to your representing him/her, key questions to ask, and the advance you would like to achieve. Make sure your expectations about the advance are realistic. Know before you go. As long as you are making progress, you are doing fine. Selling legal services is not the way to get immediate gratification; it can take a while.

HOW TO NETWORK INSIDE AND OUTSIDE THE FIRM

The single most overlooked opportunity for associates is right in their own firms. You must be proactive in seeking out partners for many reasons: mentoring, getting the kind of work they want to do, and getting known throughout the firm for what you bring to the table.

Diversity and inclusion are serious initiatives at law firms as well as the companies that hire them. We use these terms in the most broadly defined way here. Diverse experiences, perspectives, and skill sets are embraced because they produce fresh ideas, new approaches, and better business decisions. As such, we suggest that there should be a place for associates on client teams.

Of course, partners need to network too—how else can your partners possibly introduce you to a client or contact if she doesn't know you can provide that kind of service, have an interest in a particular industry, or recently handled a relevant matter or transaction?

No lawyer should ever overlook the importance of networking with staff, both within the firm and at a client business. Too often, we have seen that lawyers arrogantly view, refer to, and treat people as "non-lawyers." Instead, recognize the administrative and business professionals in the firm as the people and professionals on whom your career is very much dependent. They are part of the team and should be thought of—and referred to—in terms of who and what they are rather than what they are not. More often than you may realize, it's these folks who might make or break you—you may not appreciate who the gatekeepers are, who holds power, and who knows whom inside or outside the firm.

Put more positively, the way you treat staff inside and outside the firm has the potential to distinguish you from many lawyers. You never know who might be able to help you.

Dennis Snow of Snow & Associates, a customer service excellence expert, says: "Think about those times in your personal life when you were grateful for something that someone did. I mean truly grateful. Remember how sincere and heartfelt your appreciation was toward that person? Can you remember the last time you showed that level of appreciation to an employee or group of employees in your organization? The need to be appreciated is one of the strongest needs of all. When employees work hard all day, doing the real work of the company, being treated with honor isn't too much to ask."

Consider the professionals who provide support to a company president or general counsel—executive assistants, paralegals, assistant counsels, executive assistants, receptionists, and so forth. When you, other lawyers in your firm, and your support staff forge and maintain good relationships with these people, you are creating more opportunities to develop business and provide the level of service required for client loyalty.

Understanding the importance of the breadth and depth of relationships is foundational. If you apply this concept to your practice, it will also help with the more sophisticated approaches and concepts involved in cross-selling and building client teams.

When you and your firm have many points of contact within a client organization, this facilitates the kinds of conversations that are the essence of client retention and cross-selling. It provides many channels of information access that can make the difference between being proactive and reactive. You will have many avenues to communicate that you do not take your client for granted. Moreover, having relationships at all levels within your client companies helps you retain them when one person leaves. And, finally, it helps insulate you and your firm from being fired when the client becomes unhappy over a minor error or a service issue.

It can be challenging to move beyond "water cooler" talk to business conversations. However, you must do this in order to gather the information that will, in turn, help you devise solutions. Here are some questions (along with the networking questions listed earlier in this chapter) that change the talk to business in just about any situation:

- What do you do?
- How did you get into your industry?
- Tell me about your business/clients/practice.
- What trends do you see?
- What do you think makes a good lawyer?

It should be apparent that these questions apply within the law firm office as well as anywhere outside of it.

There are a few things associates in a large firm can do differently. First, get to know your firm. Talk to other associates. Learn everything you can about your firm and how it operates as a business. Look at organizational charts. Familiarize yourself with the business and financial terminology. Seek out firm resources and tap into them. Find out about the level of support for marketing and selling activities in your firm.

Next, go to lunch with a mentor or a practice group (or other firm) leader. Discuss the firm's approach to marketing and business development, the role of associates, and how you can help partners meet their goals.

Schedule a meeting with someone in the marketing/business development and professional development areas to discuss resources available to you and how you can help with upcoming programs. Let your law practice group leaders, firm administration professionals, and mentors guide you. Develop a long-term plan for defining your legal identity, the services you want to provide, and how to become visible to potential clients.

Finally, build your network as you progress throughout your career. Form good practice management habits and make the time to cultivate and maintain your network in a systematic, routine manner. You will enjoy success in your marketing and sales efforts and ensure that your long-term career prospects are good.

CHAPTER FLASHBACK

- The ability to establish trust and rapport quickly is a skill that you can and must learn.
- Networking is being helpful to others. Build relationships before you need them!
- Attend industry/trade association events.
- If you already belong to associations, you must be engaged. Attend meetings regularly and get involved in committees that offer you good visibility and good opportunities for developing relationships with your targets.
- Join mailing lists and listserves on the Web. Read blogs to learn what people are saying. These are readily available tools that help you to learn more about (and stay abreast of) the industry needs within a target market.
- Carry your business cards with you at all times.
- Focus on introductions and relationships, not selling.
- Introduce new contacts to one another.
- Avoid spending a lot of time with people you already know (unless they have an opportunity to give you a cross-introduction).
- Don't offer your card until you have made a connection with the other person or established some kind of rapport.
- Spend four to nine minutes with any one individual at networking events.
- It's perfectly fine to gently extract yourself from a conversation.
- Don't sell—Listen!
- Your "elevator pitch" is your introduction and description of you. It is your opportunity to define (or redefine) your personal brand or your reputation.
- Guidelines of your elevator pitch: keep it short, think "tagline," solve a problem, point out the benefits, be excited about your work, be genuine. Practice makes perfect. Use the elevator pitch worksheet in this chapter to get started.

- One of the most important things you can do is to maintain and keep in touch with prospects, clients, and referral sources.
- Be patient: it takes an average of six to eight contacts with a prospect before closing the business.
- Touch base with all individuals in your database at least four times a year.
- Network with the people inside the firm. They are just as important as those with whom you network outside of it.
- No lawyer should ever overlook the importance of networking with staff at all levels, both within the firm and at a client's or contact's business.
- Build your network as you progress throughout your career.
- Go to lunch with a mentor or your practice group leader. Discuss the firm's approach to marketing, the role of associates, and how you can help partners meet their goals.

CHAPTER 4

Visibility: Speaking, Events, and Publishing

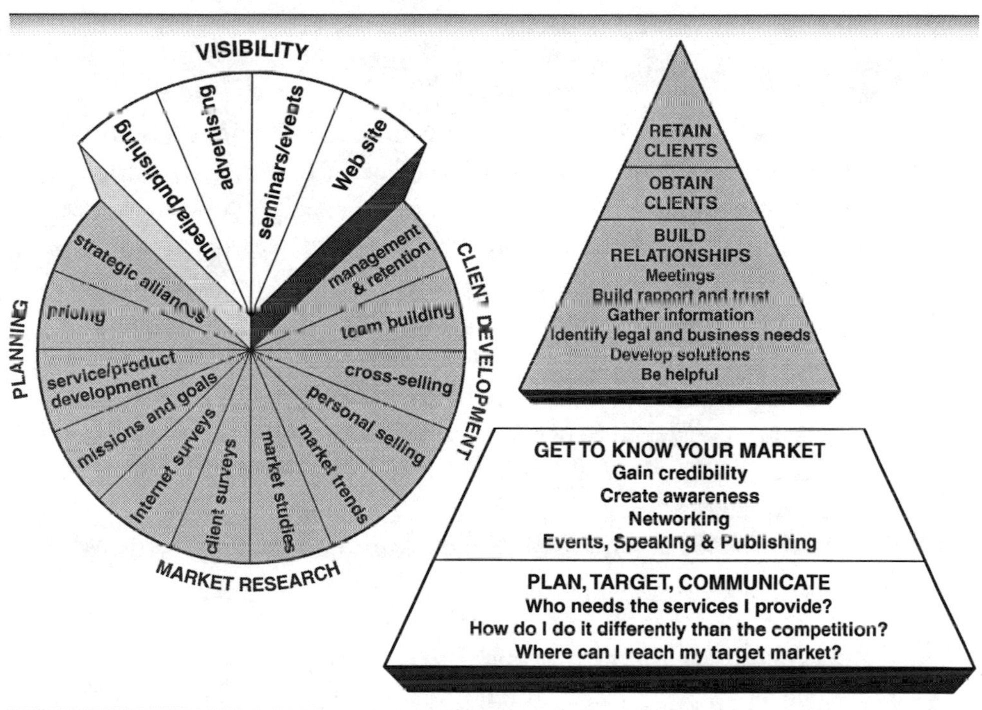

► Visibility, by definition, is the result of a range of activities that make you well-known among potential clients. Visibility builders include attending events, speaking, writing articles, and actively "showing up" at firm functions. ◄

The previous chapters' contents on networking and speaking provide you with a good background for how to get the most out of speeches and meeting people at functions and events. In this chapter, we go deeper into the business development aspects of those activities. Our goal is to help you get the maximum gains from your efforts.

Many lawyers and firms only pay attention to the opportunities presented when they are at an event or presentation, rather than before or after it. Lawyers sometimes spend a great deal of time and money on seminars and sponsorships that may not be done really well. Further, attorneys often neglect to follow up. In this chapter, we share industry best practices so that you can unlock the enormous potential created by these opportunities.

SPEAKING

Giving speeches—that is, providing substantive information on topics that are important to buyers of legal services, and delivering it with style—is highly effective. Seminars and speaking engagements give attendees the chance to "preview" you and see you as knowledgeable, learn about legal and business issues, and meet others with whom they have common interests.

Law firms are not (and should not strive to be) in the seminar business. However, seminars can and should be done in your offices for a select, qualified audience. This allows for intimacy, impressions of exclusivity and value, and delivery of tailored information that is meaningful to everyone in the group. They are great marketing and sales vehicles. We recommend this over an approach that involves somewhat randomly selecting a topic and then spending time trying to drum up attendance.

Another suggested format is to offer training or other presentations to clients, prospects, and referral sources around an identified need or concern at their office. This is often expected of outside counsel with significant client relationships, but it is also appreciated. It provides a nice way to deepen relationships, add value beyond specific matters, meet more people within an organization, and continue to elicit needs.

For associates as well as partners, teaming up with a third party provider to offer these programs can be a real boost. Besides adding content and authority, you will double your list of prospective attendees. Another good way to gain experience and raise your visibility inside the firm is to deliver a presentation for your own or a different practice group. It will also encourage client-facing lawyers to think of you as a potential member of a client team.

When done well, seminars are platforms for you to demonstrate your experience and abilities with people. Seminars also provide relationship-building opportunities, but only if you do that which is required to create them. A speech does not, in and of itself, do that much for you. Your audience has high standards—an excellent presentation is expected, so it's just not enough to accomplish the mission.

CHECKLIST: What to Do with Your Presentation

- Turn your presentation into an article (and vice versa).
- Post your presentation on your Web site. Link to it from your biography.
- Maintain a list of your program titles, dates, and locations of your speeches. Include the name of the organization for which you presented, if applicable (this does not include names of client companies, which should be kept confidential).
- Send highlights, checklists, or excerpts to your mailing list. Offer a follow-up in your program. For example, invite attendees to leave their business cards to be added to your mailing list or to receive your slides or an article that you reference in your speech.
- Notify press contacts that you will be giving a speech. Send them an outline so they can see what you will be covering. Invite them to attend so they have a chance to see you in action. Make it interesting and relevant to a current event or news story.
- Submit upcoming programs that are open to the public to publications' calendars of events contacts.

THE PROCESS FOR MAXIMIZING ROI AND LEVERAGING OPPORTUNITIES

We asked Ronna West Cross, Esq., Director of Business Development for Patton Boggs LLP in the firm's Dallas office, to share her secrets for getting the most out of firm events and speaking engagements.

Cross insists that it isn't rocket science, but says it takes diligence before, during, and after events and speeches.

Goal: Maximize Return on Investment (ROI) for firm-sponsored events and individual speaking engagements.

Process:

Before the Event (Approximately One Week Prior)

1. *Obtain the RSVP List*

Contact the event organizer and ask for the RSVP list. If your firm is an event sponsor, attempt to negotiate the right to receive the RSVP list in advance as part of your contract with the event organizer. If you are a speaker, ask for the list as a courtesy. You can explain that you want to know who will be at the event so you can maximize your time and your firm's time spent at the event.

2. *Connect with Speakers*

If you are a speaker at the event and there are other speakers who are targets/prospects for you/your firm, invite the speaker prospects to dinner during the event. Speakers are generally more open to accepting a dinner invitation from another speaker than they are to accepting an invitation from a lawyer attendee. Make sure you have a reservation at a nice restaurant. Be prepared to cover the cost of the meal since you extended the invitation.

3. *"Due Diligence" the RSVP List*

Carefully review the attendee list. Determine who is a good prospect for you and/or your firm. Create a spreadsheet that lists your prospects. We typically create a spreadsheet that includes columns for the prospect name and company, whether the prospect is an existing firm client, background information on the prospect and company, and a blank column for notes during the event. Taking contemporaneous notes at the event will be of tremendous value when you return to your desk and begin following up. It is virtually impossible to remember every conversation you had, so write it down as often and inconspicuously as possible.

4. *Work the List*

Cross-reference the list with your firm's client base to determine which organizations or individuals are already firm clients. If there are existing clients on the list, find out who in your firm manages the relationship. Meet with that lawyer and get as much background information as possible. Ask what matters your firm handles for the client. Ask about personalities. Ask about current issues facing the company. Any information you obtain will make you more comfortable talking with the prospect at the event. Arm yourself so you can be at ease when you make the connection.

5. *Do Your Research*

If you have time (if you don't, make time anyway), research and educate yourself about your target companies. Review the press on the company Web sites. Search for background information on the Internet. Digest as much as you can about the person and company before you meet them. People love it when you have taken the initiative to learn about them. It's flattering and reflects well on how proactive you would be as their counsel.

6. *Create a "Hit List"*

You have limited time at the event. Use it wisely; i.e., use your time to develop relationships with people that can and are likely to hire you/your firm. As an aside, your colleagues DO NOT fit in this category, so do not spend your time talking and "clumping" with them.

To maximize the return on the time spent with event attendees, create "hit lists" for events. Your hit list can include only one person or it can have several. You may realize that the dream client you've been eyeing will be at the event. It's okay if that's the only person on your list. You may need the entire event to track him/her down and strike up a conversation. If you have several dream clients on your list, rank them by priority. You want your best prospect at the top of the list. Take your time and find him/her.

As Director of Business Development, Cross has her own hit list for every event. She also ensures that she knows the targets on her team members' hit lists. This enables her to work the room for everyone. If she encounters someone who wasn't on her list, but she knows that a lawyer on her team wants to meet that person, she finds her team member and makes the introduction. Patton Boggs lawyers have become very effective at working event rooms as a result of these actions.

7. *What if I can't get the RSVP List?*

Course materials typically include the RSVP list for course attendees. Agendas for conferences will have the topics and speaker lists.

Event Web sites sometimes publish the attendee list at the last minute.

Use whatever information you can get to learn who will be at the event in advance, and then do as much due diligence as you can.

At the Event

Stick to your hit list and work the room. Be judicious about how you spend your time at the event. Be prepared with ways to extract yourself from a conversation.

Cross brings her hit list on a paper the size of a business card. That way, she can keep it handy and refer to it easily and discreetly.

She likes to touch base with any existing clients first. This protects our current revenue stream and lets existing clients know that we value them. It also creates a nice way to ease into event networking. Talking with people you know in the beginning (again, NOT your colleagues) is comfortable and gets you into the networking mindset. Remind yourself that you are not there to sell; you're there to begin developing or further develop your relationship with current and prospective clients. Enjoy the conversation and look for ways to leave the follow-up in your court.

Ask questions and LISTEN. Listen for what's new at the company; listen for problems that have arisen; listen for opportunities to do work for the client in practice areas outside your area of expertise. This is where your due diligence comes into play. Ask about current events. Drop a line about recent press you've read on the company. Learn as much as you can. Social events (as opposed to office visits) are much more casual, and more information is often shared in the festive event environment.

Periodically capture any follow-up action items and details from conversations. Commit to making notes at regular intervals at the event. This will pay off tenfold when you are back at your desk the next day executing your follow-up.

After the Event

It's the plight of every lawyer. You go to the event and execute your plan. Then you return to your desk the next day and emergencies, routine work, and return calls await you. The temptation is to dive back into the waiting work. Resist it. Take the time to set the next steps in motion. This is where the rubber meets the road. It is also what separates the rainmakers from the rest of the crowd.

You absolutely, positively have to follow up as soon as possible. If you cannot do it the next day, make sure you do it in the same week. To make sure she meets this goal, Cross blocks out time on the day after the event to execute the follow-up. Doing all the front-end legwork, then dropping the ball in the follow-up stage is simply unacceptable.

Continue to stay in touch. Once you've done the initial follow-up, calendar to touch base the next month. Invite the prospect to lunch. Again, the more you focus on developing the relationship, the less daunting reaching out and asking for meetings becomes. Keep entering successive follow-up reminders on your calendar. Similar to dating, developing a relationship with a potential client takes time, attention, and patience. We cannot emphasize the patience portion enough. There is no substitute for consistent, sincere follow up. Eventually, the person you met at XYZ event will have a matter that's appropriate for you or your firm to handle. That's when your time and diligence will pay off, and your prospect will call you to handle the work.

Outcome

This process (which has been even further refined) has proven highly effective at Patton Boggs and has resulted in several clients across a variety of practice areas and industries.

PUBLISHING

Authoring articles is a sure way to increase visibility and build credibility as a young lawyer. For many lawyers, writing is preferable to speaking or media interviews because it allows them the opportunity to reflect and change their material before making it publicly available. Our first piece of advice is to co-author with a partner in your firm. This affords you opportunities to work with a partner in your firm and learn more about a specific issue, industry, practice area, case, or that particular partner.

We've created some tips to help you maximize the time you spend writing.

TIPS *Don't write an article and then try to place it in a publication. First obtain the editorial calendar. The editorial calendar for each trade journal you read is set annually. You want to write only an abstract that coincides with a topic on the editorial calendar and then contact the editorial staff. If you have a marketing department, submit your abstract or idea to them BEFORE you write the article. This practice helps the editorial and marketing staff understand that you are easy to work with, and they will keep you in mind as other opportunities arise.*

- Write for business publications as well as legal journals. Note editorial calendars, focus issues, guidelines, and deadlines.
- Order reprints of your article and use it as a handout at speeches or in presentations.
- Use the reprint as a mailing to all or some of the people in your contact database. An article published in a business publication or trade journal helps build credibility and visibility. Include a handwritten note on your cover letters to top prospects explaining why the article might be particularly relevant to them.
- Use it as a follow-up tool when meeting with a prospective client.
- If you are with a small office, you may place the reprints in the lobby for guests to read when visiting your firm.
- Post the article to your Web site (but ensure that you aren't violating the publication's copyrights). Add the name of the article and publication to your bio. If you are able to obtain an electronic file of your article (text or a PDF reprint), we suggest linking the article within your online biography.
- Turn the article into a speech.
- Add your contact information in the article so readers are able to contact you.
- Publish your photo with your article, if possible. People think they know you better when they know what you look like. (This is another reason why a professionally-done photo is a must).
- If you can't coauthor with a partner, try writing an article with clients, colleagues, and other professional service providers. ◄

CHAPTER FLASHBACK

- *Before the event:*
  1. Obtain the RSVP list.
  2. If you are a speaker at the event and there are other speakers who are targets/prospects for you/your firm, connect with them for dinner beforehand.
  3. "Due Diligence" the RSVP List
  4. Cross-reference the list with your firm's client base to determine which organizations or individuals are already firm clients (and run a conflict check to determine any that might pose conflicts).
  5. If you have time (if you don't, make time anyway), research and educate yourself about your target companies.
  6. Create a "Hit List"

- *At the event:*
  1. Stick to your hit list and work the room.
  2. Touch base with any existing clients first.
  3. Listen for problems that have arisen; listen for opportunities to do work for the client in practice areas outside your area of expertise.

- *After the event:*
  1. Follow up as soon as possible.
  2. Block out the time of day after the event to execute the follow-up.
  3. Continue to stay in touch.

- Order reprints of your article.
- Use the reprint as a mailing to your contacts.
- Use it as a follow-up tool when meeting with a prospective client.
- If you are with a small office, you may place the reprints in the lobby for guests to read when visiting your firm.

CHAPTER 5

Before a Meeting

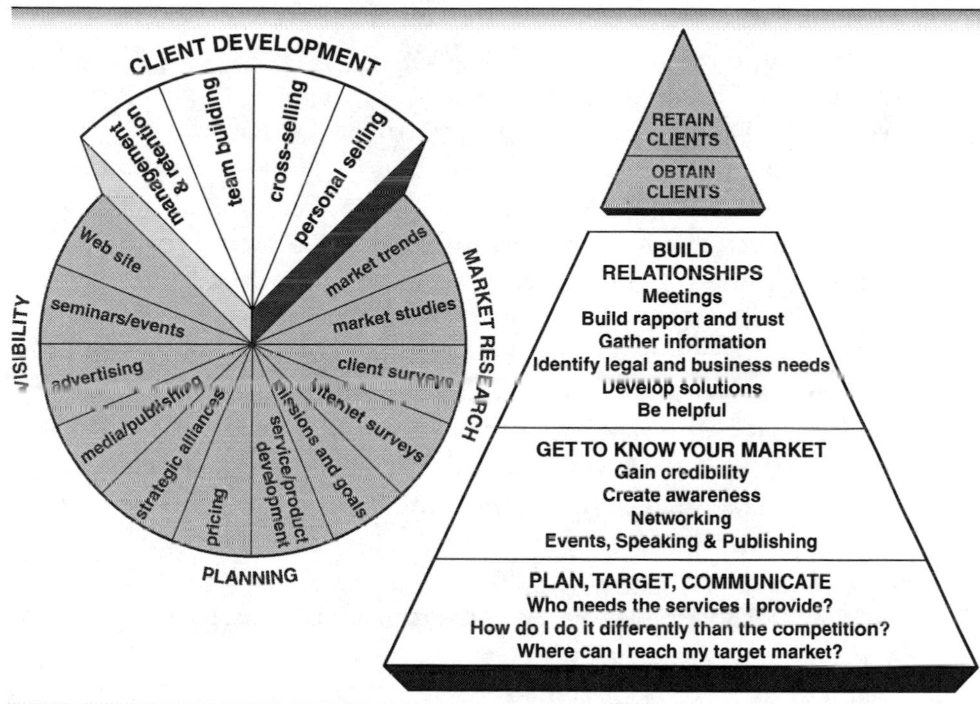

► *"Hi, Sarah! It's Alex. I'm so glad we caught you in your office. We're in the car on our way to the Kenna Company and you know how we really want that business. Since you're the first person in the marketing department I was able to reach, I'm hoping you can give us some advice about the meeting—you know how important this is to us."* ◄

Regrettably, this scenario plays more often in real life than we'd like to report. Yes, you really do need to prepare for your meetings. Do not wing it. Would you go to a closing or a deposition unprepared? The same discipline must be applied at this stage of the sales cycle. We think some associates are well suited to help manage this phase of the process.

PLANNING FOR A CLIENT MEETING

While you may have a fair amount of knowledge about the client or prospect and their needs, you are still in information-gathering mode. Your initial meeting is NOT for you to present what you can do for them. Even when you are invited to a meeting to pitch your services, you must still treat the opportunity as the early stage it really is. Remember, stay tuned into the client, whose station is always set to "WII FM: What's In It For Me?"

Meet with all lawyers from your firm who will attend the meeting. Decide how you will approach the meeting together. Remember that your actions will speak more about 1) your ability to deliver as a team, and 2) how you will work with the client than your words—and marketing materials—ever will.

This demonstrates some of the benefits of including associates on client teams. In addition to the relationship development piece, clients demand value, efficiency and, most of all, cost-effectiveness. There is abundant industry research to support this assertion. Partner-only teams do not convey that the firm recognizes what clients say they care about. We have prepared teams that are as small as two and as large as dozens. Nearly every time we have worked with teams that have assigned associates a specific role at a meeting the associates' contributions have contributed significantly to creating a positive impression.

It is helpful to know the names of everyone with whom you will be meeting. If possible, also get their titles and be familiar with their areas of responsibility, whether they've been in the news lately, and so forth. As mentioned in Chapter 4, do not assume who has the buying power or who are the influencers. Just because someone does not appear to have a high rank is no reason to jump to any conclusions about their importance and how they might affect the outcome of the hiring process. Also, ask whether there is anyone else at the company you might ask to meet while you are there, and make sure to request a tour.

Don't give in to the temptation of selling at this meeting; you will short-circuit the sales cycle. You will hurt your long-term chances of success if you develop solutions and present them right off the bat—it prevents you from getting the advance at many levels. Most importantly, it will deprive you of the opportunity to confirm your understanding of the prospect's needs afterward.

As we indicated in Chapter 2 in the section on Written Materials and How to Use Them, you should leave your brochures and bios back at the office. When you bring materials to an initial meeting (unless specifically requested to do so), it positions you as presumptuous, since you are saying that you know what the client needs even before you ask. It is more likely than not that a prospect or client has a different need or series of needs than you anticipated. You won't know until you ask, so don't paint yourself into a corner unnecessarily by limiting the solutions you might present prematurely.

CHECKLIST: Planning for a Meeting with a Prospective Client

- ✔ Gather the people from your firm with whom you will attend the meeting.
- ✔ Review the information that has been gathered.
- ✔ Determine the purpose of the meeting.
- ✔ Be informed about who will attend from the prospect's side.
- ✔ Draft an agenda and/or list of questions.
- ✔ Assign specific questions and responsibilities to everyone on the team. Make sure that everyone has an obvious role and reason for attending (that means don't bring women lawyers for the sake of having a token woman at the meeting).
- ✔ Schedule a debriefing session where you will review what happened at the meeting and plan your follow-up activities and timelines.

- Practice any transitions—the way you behave as a team speaks more loudly than anything you will say about how you and your firm have a culture of "teamwork."

These basic requirements are also critical for lawyers who are going solo into any meeting with a prospective client or referral source. The same rules essentially apply. Decide what you want to accomplish as well as any information you need to gather, review, and/or discuss beforehand.

HOW TO BE PREPARED FOR ANY MEETING

To make sure you are confident, efficient, and productive, you should prepare for your meetings. Always take the time to establish an agenda. Another way to be ready for any meeting is to anticipate objections and obstacles so that you can predetermine how to overcome them. Capture into one document all the questions and issues you can think of, especially the ones you don't want to address.

Once you have the difficult questions in writing, draft your answers. Get any data you need to have a strong reply and practice the delivery of your responses. Incidentally, this is also an excellent exercise for any speaker to do before a presentation. When you are prepared and confident, it shows.

HOW TO QUALIFY AND ASSESS

Because associates don't always have a chance to bring in business, it is hard to turn down clients. Beware: you must carefully guard your time in this area. Not all clients are "good" clients and not all prospects are either.

Defining what makes a prospect a "good" one is easier, of course, when you are able to refer back to the goals in your business plan. In short, a "good" prospect or client is one that helps you achieve one or more of the goals in your business plan.

You might decide a prospect isn't good for any number of reasons. Some prospects are simply not in the business or industry that either interests you or furthers your goals. In that case, you and they are both better off with a referral to someone who will find them to be a perfect client. Then you help yourself as well as a prospect and a referral source.

NOT ALL CLIENTS ARE GOOD FOR YOUR HEALTH

One way to combat dissatisfaction as well as reduce stresses and demands is to do things you enjoy. It sounds simple, but you do have a choice about the people with whom you work. Choose those who offer you the right level of professional challenges and interesting work. Above all, try to work with people who sincerely appreciate you and the services you provide.

In order to determine whether the prospect is "good" or not, you must be able to qualify and assess them in terms of what is important to you and your firm, both in the near and long term. For this, use predetermined criteria that are both objective and subjective. Don't settle all the time. This is your life and your career.

To qualify a prospect, check your CRM or send an email to your colleagues in the firm that asks if anyone else has relationships with the company and/or person. Do this *before meeting with the prospect* to help you determine whether to pursue the relationship. If you are a solo practitioner, send an email to your referral network of other professional service providers.

You may also use information resources to qualify a prospect. There are many excellent commercial databases available with a range of data available—competitive intelligence and knowledge management are big business in the legal industry and with good reason. Try searching the Web to conduct market research on the individual(s) with whom you are meeting (as well as any competitors). A good tool is www.google.com. Simply type the individual's name in the search field. (While you're at it, do a Google search of your own name to see what surfaces about you.) *The Lawyer's Guide to Fact Finding on the Internet, Third Edition* (ABA, 2006) is an excellent resource for tips on researching people and firms.

We always encourage lawyers to create an agenda with the prospective client *before* the meeting. Ask the prospect what he or she would like to discuss before the meeting so that you are best prepared.

▶ Many lawyers report feeling dissatisfied with their working and personal lives. The demands and stresses on lawyers are high. Perhaps this is why lawyers are particularly prone to depression, with recent data showing an alarming increase in the numbers in the profession who are suffering from it. The ABA offers lawyer assistance programs. If you or a colleague needs help, please locate resources by visiting www.abanet.org/legalservices/colap/ (the ABA Commission on Lawyers Assistance Programs). Your state or local bar association may also have a lawyers assistance program. ◀

Another good idea is to determine what will be the end time of the meeting so that you can both plan accordingly and demonstrate your abilities to be respectful of others' time and work within a specific time frame.

You must visit the company's Web site before your meeting. You may learn a great deal by reading articles, press releases from the "newsroom," or other sections containing media. We heard a terrific point made by a general counsel who didn't hire a lawyer and his firm based on the simple facts that they hadn't visited his company's Web site nor subscribed to a free offering there.

Those on the short list of qualified buyers can continue to progress through the sales cycle and move to the next stage. Keep advancing and move your potential client closer to an engagement. Schedule another meeting, get introduced to someone new, or provide a list of references. The relationship building stage of the sales cycle is the longest, as lawyers must sometimes have many meetings with qualified prospects and clients as they aim for a steady stream of advances toward new engagements.

You want a prospective client who looks for "fit" as well as substance. This is the whole reason for you to go through the process of qualifying and assessing. Unless you have a true niche, there are plenty of smart lawyers with the ability to do the same work as you on a substantive level. Just as clients want to work with a lawyer who understands their business and what is important to them, you want to work with a client who appreciates YOU. Remember, you're going for a long-term relationship here.

During your meeting, your role is to try to understand what the prospect or client thinks their business and legal needs are—and address the same. Many times lawyers try to sell a solution to an issue that the client doesn't know exists or doesn't think is important.

How much time should be spent on all this analysis? That's a very difficult question, especially for lawyers. Many would rather stay in the office reviewing industry, financial, and other types of data than go out and start selling. There is always the risk (and, in our view, a real tendency) of putting too much time into this because there is always more to learn.

We have worked with many lawyers who are stuck in "analysis paralysis." Don't let this happen to you—you DO NOT need to gather and review mountains of minutiae before you approach a client, close the business, and begin doing work for them. The need for all this data is sometimes really an excuse to not have to approach a prospect. If that is the case, then recognize it as an obstacle you have created and remove it. Get out of your own way.

CHAPTER FLASHBACK

- Prepare for your meetings—don't wing it.
- Your initial meeting is NOT for you to present what you can do for others.
- Qualify. It's your life—decide what kinds of people and work you want in your career. Do things and be around others you enjoy. This reduces stress and demands.
- The relationship-building stage of the sales cycle is the longest.
- Find prospective clients who look for "fit" as well as substance.
- Understand what prospects think their business and legal need is—and address the same. Do not raise issues that the client doesn't know exist or doesn't think is important.

CHAPTER 6

At the Meeting

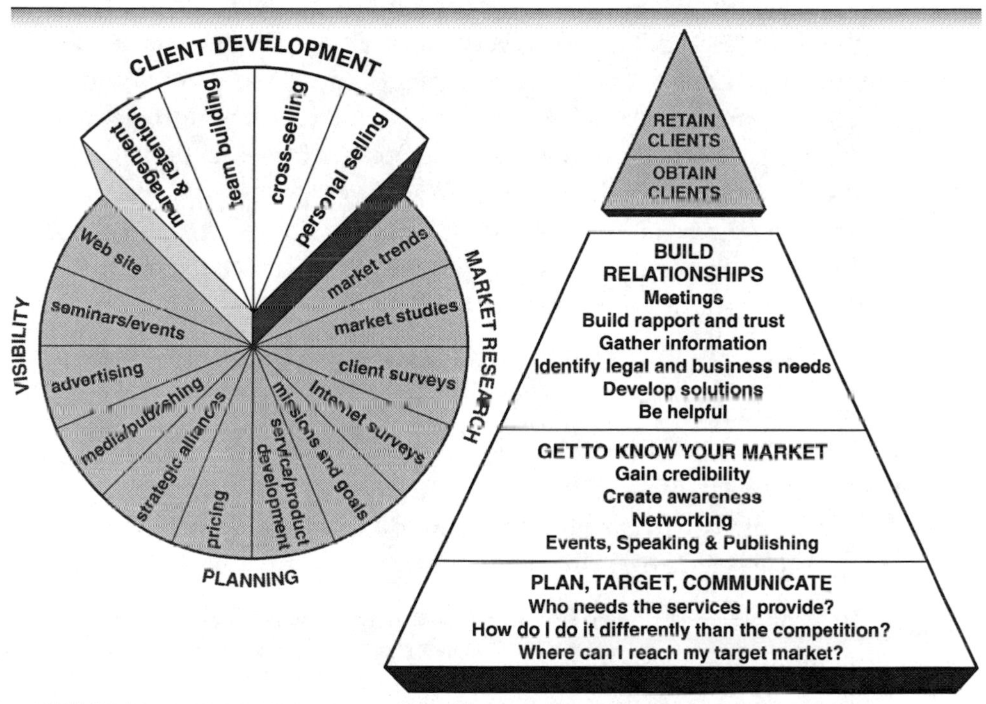

WHEN MEETING WITH A PROSPECT OR CLIENT

► Now that you have prepared for your scheduled meeting, you're ready to go. There are some key areas that will enhance your relationship and communications when you're meeting with your prospects and clients. ◄

First, learn how to identify your buyer's learning style and personality type. Pay attention to your (and their) nonverbal communications. Watch your body language when meeting prospects. For example, don't lean back, cross your arms, or turn sideways—these actions will make you appear guarded. Lean forward a bit, sit centered, and make eye contact.

Next, use your "What to Bring to a Meeting" checklist in this chapter to stay organized and confident. It will help you cover all the bases. Many lawyers seem to wrestle with what to bring to the meeting. Usually, there is some strange compulsion to bring a full firm brochure and everything about everyone as well as all that they have written or has been written about them. You do not need this crutch; you know that it is a mistake to compete with your marketing materials. If you insist on bringing materials with you, don't distribute them until the end of the meeting. (We discussed this earlier in the book—please refer to Chapter One.)

The most important thing is to never leave a meeting with a prospect without offering a valuable follow-up.

- "I wrote an article on this very topic; if you'd like, I can email it to you."
- "I know of someone who may be interested in your product; would you like an introduction?"
- "Would you like me to add you to our mailing list so that you receive alerts regarding employment?"

A corollary to this is that you don't want to leave a meeting without a follow-up and a timeframe.

- "What do you think the next step should be?"
- "When should we touch base again?"
- "If you send me the documents you have, I'll review them and get back to you by the end of the week."
- "What would you like to have happen? When?"

This way, there is clarity about what is to happen next and when that will be.

Finally, qualify and assess at all times. Learn the basic facilitation skills covered in this chapter to continue to elicit information throughout the meeting, keep it running smoothly, and leave with the advance.

CHECKLIST: What to Take with You to the Meeting

- Agenda–it's better to send it in advance
- Purpose–know why you are going
- Good questions (see the WJF Institute's "20 Questions You Should Ask Your Current and Prospective Clients")
- Background information
- Notepad
- Pen
- Business cards–bring several
- Most importantly, your listening ears!

CHECKLIST: The WJF Institute's "20 Questions You Should Ask Your Current and Prospective Clients"

We've both had the privilege of participating in Bill Flannery's sales training program offered by the WJF Institute. Flannery was an original and remains a master of law firm sales. We find that we have consistently used the information, tactics, and skills learned in those sessions each week in our law firms. You can find these questions and terrific articles online at www.wjfinstitute.com. Also refer to Flannery's book *The Lawyer's Field Guide to Effective Business Development.*

1. What do you want your organization to look like in one year, two years, or five years?
2. When and where do you plan to open new offices or plants?
3. What new products, services, or major changes are you anticipating?
4. What kind of research and development do you see as necessary for you to meet your strategic objectives?
5. What is the profile of your typical customer?
6. What are your employee relations concerns?

- ✓ 7. Who are your main competitors?
- ✓ 8. What has the financial climate been like for your business?
- ✓ 9. How are you organized, what does your organization chart look like, and who are the key executives?
- ✓ 10. How are decisions made, and who are the decision-makers?
- ✓ 11. What is the leadership style here?
- ✓ 12. Is there a legal department, how is it organized, and what is its role?
- ✓ 13. What do you see outside counsel accomplishing for you or your organization?
- ✓ 14. What recent uncertainties are affecting your business, or what changes of any sort have particularly concerned you recently?
- ✓ 15. What sort of legal services are you currently using, and do you expect any changes?
- ✓ 16. What do you like about what other firms do, and what do you wish they would do differently?
- ✓ 17. How much detail do you like to get from your lawyers?
- ✓ 18. How do you perceive our firm in particular?
- ✓ 19. What criteria do you use in selecting lawyers? What makes a good lawyer?
- ✓ 20. How does your budgeting for legal services compare to what you spend on other resources?

LEARNING STYLES

People do learn and process differently. To be an effective communicator, you should be able to deliver information in ways that make it easiest for people of whatever learning style to process and understand. While people may not have purely one style, everyone has a definite preference for one style more than another.

The three distinct learning styles are visual, auditory, and kinesthetic. Many people employ elements of more than one style. Your clues as to which style your prospect or client has will be voice, gestures, word selection, and eye movement.

- **Visual:** Processes with pictures, mental images. Typical phrases: "*I see, I can't picture it, In view of, It's not clear to me, We don't see eye to eye . . .*" Their eyes will move up and to your right when you ask them questions—they are visualizing their answers.
- **Auditory:** Processes with words, sounds. Listen to see if they have a well-modulated voice. Typical phrases: "*I hear you, To tell the truth, Clear as a bell, Let's talk, Rings a bell, Just doesn't sound right . . .*" Their eyes will shift down and to your left. Sometimes they will tilt an ear upward—they are listening.
- **Kinesthetic:** Processes with feeling-based, physical memory. They are expressive and their gestures tend to match what they're saying. Typical phrases: "*My gut feeling is, Slipped my mind, It's a hassle, Start from scratch, Pull some strings, Can't get my arms around it, Boils down to . . .*" Their eyes tend to shift down and to your right as if trying to recall a feeling.

Mirroring and matching your prospect's body language is a technique that helps you to quickly establish trust and rapport—remember that people buy from people with whom they are comfortable, know, and like. You can learn this, but you must practice in order to not appear as though you are mimicking the person. The mirroring must be subtle. If it's obvious, your prospect will think you are either making fun or just being manipulative.

In other words, if you are a visual learner, then be aware of how you are communicating with a prospective client who is either auditory or kinesthetic. Consciously match your tone of voice, body language, expressions, and actions to the other person. This makes it easier for him/her to process any information you might be trying to give.

This is important and powerful to know because people reward people with styles that are similar to their own. For those who want a more in-depth education, there are plenty of resources on Neuro Linguistics Programming (NLP)™ available. Again, this information is to be used only to improve your communications and never to manipulate anyone.

We find that it is enough for lawyers to be aware of the basics; since a majority of lawyers are visual learners, it helps to be cognizant of other styles. This is particularly true for lawyers who sometimes are more focused on word selection than their body language or tone of voice. Some studies report slightly different percentages, but the "What Communicates?" chart below provides good baselines.

PERSONALITY TYPES

Just as it is helpful to know people's learning styles, it is also helpful to identify their personality types. There are four personality types:

- **Driver:** These types of buyers are net-net. They are all business. Time is money, so plan for a short meeting. Be concise when dealing with them (think bullet points and bottom line). Let them be the boss.
- **Analytical:** These types of buyers are thinkers. They don't make decisions as quickly as people with any of the other styles. They don't like risk. Provide supporting documents/evidence throughout the process and don't be aggressive. No pushing!
- **Amiable:** These types of buyers are easygoing but do not respond well to pressure. Make them comfortable with guarantees and take the time to build a personal relationship.

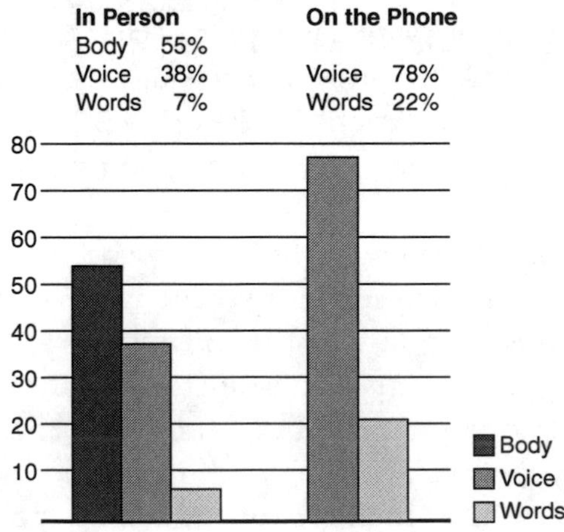

- **Expressive:** These types of buyers are outgoing and communicate with a lot of body language. React positively to their ideas, provide them with references, and give a fast-paced presentation.

THE DEPOSITION RULE

Try to remember the "deposition rule" when meeting with prospects and clients. In a deposition the lawyer asking questions is in control. To remain in control of your sales meeting with a prospect, adhere to the deposition rule of 80/20. When meeting a prospect, listen 80 percent of the time and talk 20 percent of the time, not only to develop the relationship, but also to gather the information that helps you understand his/her needs.

More specifically, ask your clients and prospects "smart questions" to be well equipped to assess (and later address) their needs. Below are a few, and you can supplement with some of the networking questions listed in Chapter 3.

- Tell me about your business.
- How did you get into your industry?
- What is your 3-year goal for your company?
- How will the decision regarding legal services be made?
- How do you like to work with a lawyer/law firm?

CHAPTER FLASHBACK

- Identify your buyer's learning style and personality type.
- Next, use your "What to Bring to a Meeting" Checklist in this chapter to stay organized and confident.
- The most important thing is to never leave a meeting with a prospect without offering a valuable follow-up.
- Mirroring and matching your prospect's body language is a technique that helps you to establish trust and rapport quickly.

CHAPTER 7

Asking for Business and Setting Expectations

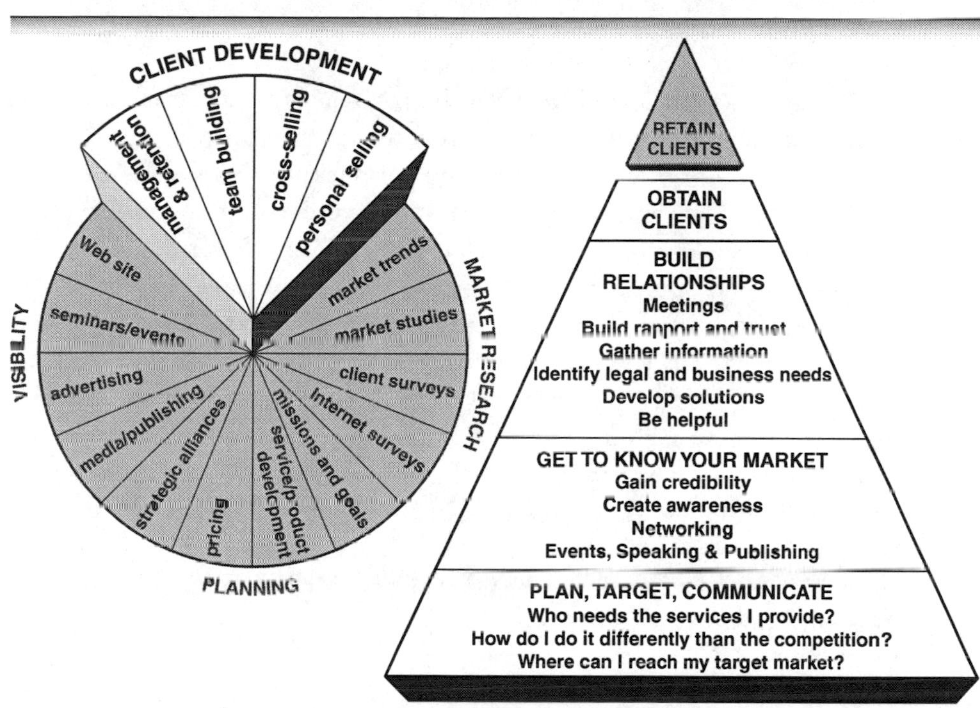

- At this point in the relationship, you have
  - planned, targeted, and communicated;
  - researched, met, and gotten to know your target market;
  - increased your visibility and credibility;
  - built rapport and trust;
  - identified needs; and
  - developed solutions ◄

Now, finally, it is time to "ASK" for business and obtain the client. Lawyers seem to find this to be the single most excruciating task in the entire process. To become more comfortable, zero in on why you are so reluctant to ask. Usually, you haven't yet shifted your thinking about selling. Try this tip:

TIP ► Don't think of it as asking someone to do you a favor and hire you. Think of it as offering a solution or help to someone who has a problem. ◄

Plenty of people spend time developing relationships, but don't feel at ease asking for business. When you have been helpful to others, at some point, they will appreciate your asking them to let you work on their legal and business issues; they understand and appreciate that this is just another way that you are being helpful.

Moreover, if you have asked good questions, listened carefully and have real solutions to offer, then "closing" is easy. Too many lawyers want to move from meeting someone to getting hired in the same meeting (and skip everything else!). It takes commitment and discipline to stay top of mind with potential clients so that when a legal need arises he/she will think of you. But if you do, you build a client base and referral network that brings you personal and professional success.

In short, know how and when to ask someone if you may represent him/her.

DEVELOPING SOLUTIONS

The point of developing relationships and eliciting needs is so that you can think of solutions for prospects and clients. The more strategic and creative you are, the better, since you probably have competition. Besides, most clients appreciate working with lawyers who take a "partnering" approach. Be careful not to overcomplicate things. Complex solutions may be translated by clients and prospects as over-lawyering.

To develop and present solutions that sell, first brainstorm. List every possible solution you think applies, even the most elementary or remote. Then, decide which solution(s) are best for that particular prospect or client, taking into account everything you know. Finally, find some way to go the extra mile. The "wow!" factor doesn't need to be extreme to be effective. It is more important to present solutions that are elegant in their simplicity.

For example, if the client's need is to incorporate his business, then develop a chart that shows the main differences between different entity structures. It need not be a slick piece developed by a graphic designer. Put the entities at the top, making columns with headings such as "LLP" and "S Corp," and then write short descriptions of the differences among them in each column.

It should be evident that, based on the stated need, the solution is not to simply file papers. The solution is to help clients understand the effects, both long and short term, of the decisions they are making. This approach resonates with clients, since you are reflecting back what they think the issue is and offering them options. Don't be afraid to suggest the alternative you think is best. Clients get frustrated with lawyers who can only offer "on the one hand, on the other hand" advice—they also want and expect your opinion. They are looking to you for options and direction.

HOW TO ASK FOR BUSINESS

How to ask for business is up to each individual—one size does not fit all—and it will likely be different each time. Try these as a starting point and find your own way of asking:

"I'd like the opportunity to work with you to help you resolve this issue."

"May we work together on your next matter?"

"Do you have a list of lawyers you turn to in the event of a conflict with your current law firm? How may I be considered for that list?"

The only wrong way to obtain a new client is *not* to ask for business. The answer will be "Maybe," "No," or "Yes."

"Maybe"

If there is some resistance to hiring you, then take the time to understand the reasons. This requires delicate probing. Ask questions to get the clarification you need. Often, digging in a bit will allow you to relieve a prospect from a concern or misguided information. Generally, when lawyers are told "you are too expensive," "your rates are too high," "your firm is smaller than the firms we generally use" or "people here at Acme Manufacturing haven't heard of your firm," they erroneously translate the responses to mean "WE ARE NOT GOING TO HIRE YOU." These responses may not be the real reasons or the obstacles you perceive. Treat them as opportunities to learn more so that you can address the true concerns.

The reason lawyers aren't comfortable asking for business is because they don't want the rejection. Because of this, they sometimes give up too easily or too early. This does avoid the possibility of rejection. But it also results in unnecessary failure.

Don't give up—ask questions and learn more about what are the real objections to you or your firm. Learning to overcome obstacles during conversations can change hesitation and "no" into "yes" more often than not. When a prospect is unsure as to whether there is a good fit, it is your opportunity to showcase your talent, value and differentiator. When you are met with an obstacle (or what sales professionals call "objections"), take the time to talk through it with your client, prospect, or referrer.

The process of overcoming objections in sales is broken down into three stages:

1. Isolate
2. Clarify
3. Negotiate

To demonstrate how the process is applied in reality, let's take an example from above and apply the three steps:

Prospect: "Your firm is smaller than the firms we generally use."

You (Isolate—try to determine the exact hesitation): "Are you concerned that a firm our size can't staff the deal?"

Prospect: "Yes. That is my concern."

You (Clarify): "How many people work on your deals from the larger firms at one time?"

Prospect: "We usually have half a dozen attorneys working to get our deals closed on time."

You (Negotiate): "Yes, we are smaller in firm size than firms you have historically used. However, we staff our deal teams with same number. You won't have to be concerned about enough lawyers on the team. . . . Do you have other issues stopping us from working with your company?"

You still may not be hired, but at least you'll ensure that you have learned more than you knew before, and that your prospect has learned more about you.

"No"

If the answer is "no," don't take it personally. Perhaps the lawyer who obtained the business has had a long relationship with the client. Continue to stay in touch. It sounds counterintuitive, but lost business is seldom truly "lost." There is a strong likelihood you may still represent that client in the future if you focus on the relationship, not just the particular business. What happens if the lawyer the client has chosen relocates to another part of the country? Changes careers? Has a conflict? Doesn't communicate well or provide the results expected? That's right. There's a good possibility the client will call upon you, if you've continued your contact.

Developing relationships that turn into paying clients isn't a formula. The exact amount of time this takes will depend on the nature of the practice and other factors. Of course, the whole point of the sales cycle is to get to the next stage and actually obtain new engagements. That doesn't always happen the first time you ask. Be resilient and keep in touch.

"Yes"

The client has agreed to hire you. The next step is to discuss your client's expectations. Yes, even before you start the legal work. The way in which you deliver your service is just as important as the advice itself. Understanding expectations before a matter is active is critical to your ability to deliver what the client wants (see client service tips in Chapter 8).

SETTING EXPECTATIONS

Many lawyers use retainer agreements and engagement letters to communicate expectations. These documents are built around fees and formal engagement issues. The expectations we are referring to include communication, accessibility, team/staff knowledge, and so on. Businesses set expectations, too, by using Outside Counsel Guidelines, a formal document that often contacts very specific requirements.

Outside Counsel Guidelines usually address everything about the relationship, including arrangements regarding adding new lawyers to the matters, case status, fees, reporting structure, budgets, etc. The Outside Counsel Guidelines are often published. You will need to obtain different guidelines from companies in your target market to get a true understanding of the variables from organization to organization. You'll spot trends that will be valuable to you going forward.

Many clients are NOT big corporations with predetermined guidelines, so we suggest creating a rider to your client intake form:

Sample Client Expectations Rider

Billing:

- Would you prefer to be billed every 15 or 30 days?
- Would you like a copy of the bill to be sent to anyone else?
- Is there specific information you would like me to include in the service description of your bills (see tip box below for information)?

Relationships:

- Would you like to meet the other lawyers, paralegals, or staff who will be working on your case?
- When a new lawyer works on your matter, do I need preapproval from you or the company?

Communication:

- How often would you like a progress report?
- How shall we update you (phone, hard copy, email)?
- Would you like my mobile phone number in case of emergencies?
- Is there anything you'd like me to know (or want to ask me) before we begin working together?

TIPS **BILLING STATEMENTS THAT COMMUNICATE VALUE**

- **Example:**

  Pay close attention to your narrative descriptions on each bill. Lawyers and law firms spend enormous amounts of money to communicate how their value is better than the competition. Brochures, Web sites, lunches, seminars, and special events are just a few mediums in which lawyers try to get clients to listen to them. Of everything you can spend your money on the client will read one thing for certain: THE BILL.

- *Example of Frequently Used Description*

  Teleconference with client 1.0

  This doesn't communicate much of anything to the client. You must incorporate crisp descriptions of your substantive knowledge, good advice, and strong role in solving their problem.

- *Example of Proper Description*

  Teleconference discussion regarding legal ramifications of proposed contract changes by opposing counsel. 1.0

This example is preferred. It reminds the client that you navigated a potential legal pitfall for them and that you are representing and protecting them and their business. ◄

CHECKLIST: Client Service—Setting Expectations

The following is a list of suggested points critical to maintaining a strong, productive relationship with lawyers and decision makers. Clarifying each of these issues at the outset—whether through a formal Request for Proposal process or during the initiation of a specific matter—will ensure that expectations are set and met.

General Policies

- Corporate and Legal Department mission, culture, and philosophy
- Key corporate contacts
- Increasing billing rates
- Charging ancillary services and out-of-pocket expenses
- Submitting invoices
- Paying invoices
- Requesting amendments
- Selecting and managing subcontractors
- Changing key staff assignments
- Evaluating performance

Ongoing Project Management

- Defining roles and responsibilities
- Accessibility and responsiveness
- Preparing and maintaining case work plans
- Assigning in-house and outside counsel staff
- Projecting costs and budgeting
- Reporting project status
- Identifying and resolving problems
- Maintaining case files
- Establishing overall communication and management procedures

Now that you have set expectations with the client, it is time to provide him or her with solid legal advice. The next chapter focuses on how you simultaneously REPRESENT and SERVE your client.

Remember, it costs four to five times more in time and money to get a new client than it does to keep an existing one. Service is a key component of retaining your clients.

CHAPTER FLASHBACK

- If you have asked good questions, listened carefully, and have real solutions to offer, then "closing" is easier.
- Know how and when to ask someone if you may represent him/her.
- The way you won't obtain a new client for sure is *not* to ask for business.
- If the answer is "no," don't take it personally.
- Create a rider to your client intake form to learn more about your client's preferences.

CHAPTER 8

Keeping Your Client and Cross-selling

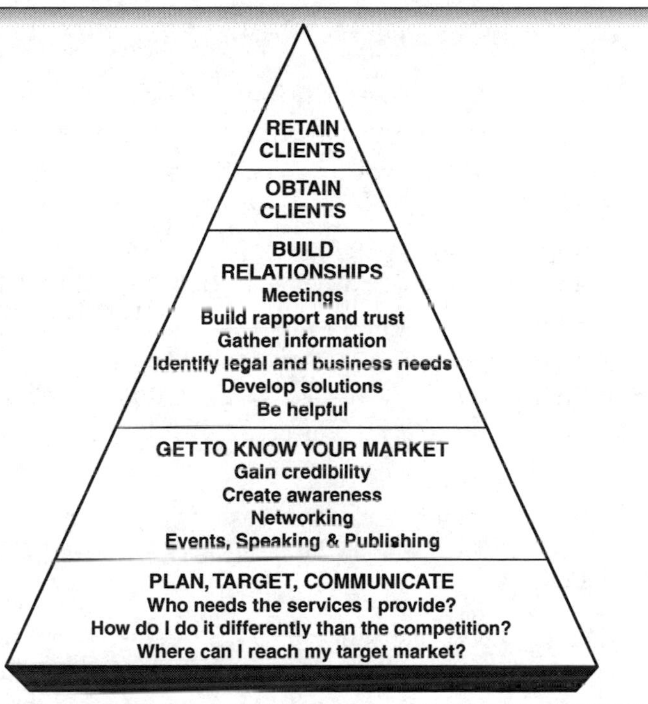

▶ While clients are getting more demanding, your competitors are getting more aggressive in their marketing and selling efforts. In a 2005 Thomson FindLaw survey, 91 percent of firms were trying to grow existing clients, and 81 percent were working to acquire new ones. Your current client is always someone else's prospect. ◀

Lawyers are paid to anticipate what can go wrong, and most are very good at it. Given all these trends, are lawyers paying enough attention to client satisfaction? ABA author Gerry Riskin[1] thinks not. "As the world becomes more competitive, there is an increasing need to nurture and protect clients from competitors. . . No law firm can take their best client for granted. . . There are just too many things going on. Should we worry? Yes. Do we worry? No."

It is a business imperative for lawyers and firms of all sizes to be serious about sales and service. Those that are will uncover incredible opportunities and create the kind of loyal clients that are rewarding to serve on every level. Those that are not may not survive.

THE LOYALTY FACTOR

By comparing the high cost of bringing in new clients versus the high profitability of a loyal customer base, the case for including client loyalty as part of your business strategy is obvious. Loyal clients make a law practice strong and solid. With loyal clients, you can usually project an ongoing revenue from clients needs, also known as annuity income. You have already read that it takes four to five times more time and energy to get a new client than it does to keep an existing one. As the client relationship strengthens, your understanding of the client makes "rates" much less relevant. Loyal clients are also great referral sources. Ask your clients for referrals from time to time.

TALKING POINT

- *"Are there other businesses, CFO's, startups, General Counsels, and local businesses (fill in the appropriate description here) you know of that I may help as well? Would you introduce me to them? I would appreciate any and all help you could give me."*

If your client is loyal, she won't hesitate for a moment. ◀

[1] Gerald A. Riskin, *The Successful Lawyer: Powerful Strategies for Transforming Your Practice* (Chicago: ABA Law Practice Management Section, 2005).

Is Your Client Loyal?

There are many interesting statistics regarding client loyalty in the legal industry. There seems to be evidence that an appalling gap exists between lawyers and their clients. For example, *Inside Counsel*'s 17th Annual Survey of General Counsel (2006) compared lawyers' ratings of client satisfaction with ratings by the clients themselves. In this survey, 52 percent of lawyers rated their client relationships as an A, but only 21 percent of their clients agreed. Similarly, 68 percent of lawyers said that the general level of legal service has improved over the last five years, but only 32 percent of clients agreed. The survey report ends with this quote from Douglas Nelson, general counsel at Croplife America: "Some outside lawyers have tremendous reputations and knowledge, but they forget that you're hiring and paying them, and that they need to keep you happy."

The pace of change is accelerating in our age of transparency, globalization, and the Internet. All clients are becoming more demanding. BTI Consulting Inc. tracks client satisfaction with law firms; in their *Key Trends in Client Relationships and Satisfaction with Law Firms: Market Opportunities for 2006* survey, they reported:

> an unprecedented drop in client satisfaction with law firms . . . Just 30.7 percent of large and Fortune 1000 companies recommend their primary law firms . . . an astonishing 53.7 percent of clients ousted their primary law firms in the past 18 months. More than 50 percent of clients also reported they plan to try at least one new law firm for substantive matters in 2006.

But consider these additional facts from that report: "exceptional client focus drives more than 40 percent of law firm recommendations" and the "BTI Client Service Doubling Factor," which is that "clients double their spending with firms clients see as best at client service."

The real litmus test is whether your clients will refer business to you or recommend you to people they know. If they do, they are loyal; this is the pinnacle of the client-lawyer/firm relationship. If they don't, they are clients you are at risk of losing. You are also going to waste a lot of time and money on generating new business over and over again. You don't need or want this churn.

If you will focus on making sure that you have satisfied clients, you have the foundation for building a solid base of what you should ultimately strive to develop: loyal clients.

CHECKLIST: How to Keep Clients Happy

It's astonishing, but many lawyers just don't devote enough time to assuring that their clients are happy by delivering excellent service. If you're one of them, change that right away. Start by brainstorming creative ideas for your practice, based on these concepts:

- ✓ Do things for free.
- ✓ Explain to clients how you are saving them money.
- ✓ Thank clients as often as you can and send handwritten notes.
- ✓ Be a pleasure to work with.
- ✓ Celebrate success.
- ✓ Return calls quickly.
- ✓ When you are meeting with clients, give them all your attention. Never allow interruptions.
- ✓ When a former client is looking for a job, help him or her network. He or she will be grateful for life.
- ✓ Avoid surprises, especially in billing statements.
- ✓ Be a great lawyer (take the Great Lawyer Test in the book's Introduction).

Client Service Is the Differentiator

The legal profession is a buyer's market. As corporations of all sizes continue to merge and industries continue to consolidate over the next few years, all signs point toward greater competition.

For individuals and law firms alike, the *2005 BTI Client Service A-Team* report identifies 17 activities that drive superior relationships; they are as follows:

1. Client focus
2. Understanding the client's business
3. Proven commitment to help

4. Providing value for the dollar
5. Unprompted communication
6. Providing a breadth of services
7. Helping to advise on business issues
8. Keeping the client informed
9. Bringing together national resources
10. Legal skills
11. Dealing with unexpected changes
12. Providing quality advice/services
13. Ability to handle problems
14. Meeting technical specifications
15. Anticipating client needs
16. International capabilities
17. Regional reputation

HOW TO USE THE END OF A MATTER AS A SALES OPPORTUNITY

A client matter has come to a close. As a lawyer prepares the file to be archived and placed in storage, all too often he will focus on wrapping up the next matter on his desk. However, the end of a transaction is one of the most opportune times to keep the dialogue open with a client and identify future revenue potential.

CHECKLIST: Selling Opportunity—The End of the Matter

- Obtain feedback: Usually clients have an opinion regarding responsiveness and availability of lawyers and staff; interpersonal skills of their legal team; value added that was provided (or not); billing procedures or the process of the deal or matter. Be sure to ask the client when expectations were reached and when they were not. Also be prepared to make changes to reflect the clients' feedback.
- Ask about future legal needs: If the clients are satisfied with recent representation, then they will be open to discussing other ways in which a firm may be able to assist them in the future, albeit in the same practice area or other practice areas in the

firm. From time to time, a firm may offer a service about which a client doesn't know.

- Identify the client's non-legal needs: A firm may be able to assist a client with a non-legal need of their day-to-day business. Perhaps a client is looking to grow its in-house capabilities and the lawyer knows of a candidate. Or maybe the lawyer has a professional contact that may have a product or service for which the client is seeking. Whatever the scenario, a client appreciates that his lawyer is thinking about business needs beyond what is billable.
- Each "End of Matter" conversation varies on the client's needs at that time, but if the conversation doesn't takes place, one may never know if the client wasn't satisfied with a firm's service or if there are other ways the lawyer/firm may help him or her in the future.

FORM: END OF MATTER QUESTIONNAIRE

TIP

▶ Any time you are asking for a rating, use an even amount of numbers (1–6 is used in this form). This will prevent any "fence-sitting" responses—they will fall on either one side or the other. ◀

This is a variation of a form used at Day, Berry & Howard LLP. Remember, it's not enough to ASK for the information—you must ACT upon it. In other words, don't ask if you aren't willing to act. How you use the feedback you collect is what makes the difference.

Your opinion is important to us. As we work to improve the quality and efficiency of our legal services, your evaluation of our services in relation to the matter described below will help us assess how well we served you on this matter and what we might do to improve our service to you in the future.

Client (you fill this in): ______________________________

Matter (you fill this in too): ______________________________

Please circle the appropriate number (ranging from 6 = excellent to 1 = poor) to indicate your opinion on each survey question.

	Excellent					Poor
1. How would you rate the legal skills of the lawyers assigned to this matter?	6	5	4	3	2	1
2. How responsive were the lawyers to your schedule and needs for this matter?	6	5	4	3	2	1
3. How well were you treated by the staff members who worked with you?	6	5	4	3	2	1
4. How well did we keep you informed of the status of this matter?	6	5	4	3	2	1
5. How satisfied are you with the result obtained in this matter?	6	5	4	3	2	1
6. How would you rate the value of the legal services you received?	6	5	4	3	2	1
7. How would you rate your overall satisfaction with the administrative aspects of working with our firm (our engagement letter, the form of our invoice, and our billing procedures)?	6	5	4	3	2	1
8. How satisfied are you with the overall performance of the firm?	6	5	4	3	2	1
9. If you need legal services again in the future, how likely are you to use our services again?	☐ Definitely will use the firm again.	☐ Probably will use the firm again.	☐ May use the firm again.	☐ Undecided at this time.	☐ Probably will not use the firm again.	☐ Definintely will not use the firm again.

10. What did you like best about our service?

____

11. What did you like least?

____

Do you have any other comments? (Include any other suggestions here or attach your own statement.)

Would you like someone to call you? ☐ Yes. ☐ No.

Name:

Telephone:

Email:

Please return this completed form to:

THANK YOU VERY MUCH FOR YOUR TIME AND YOUR FEEDBACK!

HOW TO KEEP YOUR CLIENTS

Since your client is another law firm's prospect, assign yourself retention tasks to keep your client relationships strong:

1. Visit clients at their offices rather than have meetings in yours.
2. Create client roundtables to speak to lawyers at your firm. Clients usually are comfortable talking about attributes that are important to them when working with lawyers.
3. Conduct client satisfaction interviews. Meet with clients to understand how your firm may improve services provided.
4. Introduce clients and prospects with mutual interests.
5. Get to know your clients and prospects personally. Spend time off the clock at their offices or doing something that interests both of you.
6. Bills can be utilized as a marketing tool. Include a suggestion or feedback card with your bills. Don't forget to acknowledge your client's suggestion.
7. Accessibility is important to clients. If you are not available, provide a secondary contact for client emergencies and unplanned issues.
8. Change your voicemail message frequently. We suggest every day, but at minimum, change your voice-mail message when you are going to be unavailable for a length of time: drafting

sessions, trials, and vacations. Please do not say that you are "on the phone or away from your desk." This tells your callers absolutely nothing. Also, consider providing an alternative contact if your caller needs to reach someone immediately, even if it's to return to the receptionist. Finally, everyone in the firm should follow the same format for their outgoing messages. This ensures consistency in the client's experiences with the firm.

9. When you obtain a first-time client, provide the client with a question-and-answer packet. Include a key contact list for questions regarding bills, weekend contact information, and information of other members of the firm.
10. Provide staff with a client service skills-building program annually. Recognize those who go above and beyond the call of duty.

ADDING VALUE

Your perceptions about the things that add value should be tested to make certain that your client is in agreement. If you want to know, just ask. Most clients will appreciate that you've taken the time to find out and will give you their thoughts about what they'd find helpful. For example, consider the newsletter that you are taking so much time to produce, believing that your client looks forward to getting it and gets so much out of it. It may not only go unread, it may cause your client to wonder whether you really understand what her days are like if you think she has time to read and decipher your legalese.

Client feedback, whether obtained formally or informally, will help you develop your own ways to add value for your clients. Here are some ideas to help you get started:

- If your client uses multiple firms, ask her: What special value do you see in using each firm?
- Become perceived as an expert—not just on the law, but on trends that your clients care about.
- Ask about the profile of your client's ideal customer, and then refer some prospects to him or her.

- Before every meeting and phone conference, save clients time by emailing or faxing an agenda.
- Aim to be more than your client's lawyer; aim to be a partner in growing his business.
- When you send a bill, include an explicit statement of the value your client's business received from your work.

CROSS-SELLING AND CLIENT TEAMS

While we suspect that associates may not have as many opportunities as they should to participate in client facing activities, it is unquestionable that everything done for a client eventually touches that client. Toward this end, a brief introduction to the most sophisticated aspects of sales–cross-selling and client teams–is in order.

Client teams have always been in place, but they are now being increasingly structured and the processes formalized. The time of the client service team has come. With the "me too" tendency of the industry, as firms see other firms use the client service team successfully, they are exploring it more deeply. Clients benefit from the combined experience and substantive knowledge of a well-managed team. The firm benefits by demonstrating the breadth and depth of its service offerings and gains greater access to the client's business, always expanding relationships. This offers the firm many competitive advantages.

Associates, depending on their experience level, type of firm and client, and so on, can play many roles on a team (besides being "minders and grinders"). They can be client facing. They can also make significant contributions as managers and facilitators as the team moves through the sales cycle.

CHECKLIST: Cross-selling to Existing Clients

- ✓ Select a client with several legal needs.
- ✓ Identify the responsible lawyer in your firm (avoid the term "billing attorney").
- ✓ Research what services you or your firm currently offer to this client.

- From your research, list what other services your firm may provide for this client.
- Inventory what steps are being taken to cross-sell the firm's services to this client at present.
- Find out what other law firms are working with the client.
- Gather the names of the decision-makers and key influencers at the client company.
- Arrange an internal meeting with the group of working lawyers to understand the client's recent needs and the firm's performance.
- Arrange for the responsible lawyer to meet with the client.
- Define next steps, responsibilities, and deadlines after the client meeting.

One of the most vital tools you can create for your firm or yourself is a client action plan checklist. Populate each category as outlined in the sales process with the specific resources available at your firm. Here is an example:

FORM: CLIENT ACTION PLAN CHECKLIST

Action Items		Responsible Person	Timeline	Comments/ Next Steps
Research	News clipping service Identify client needs Marketing/collateral materials needed			
Pre-Plan	Select team members			
Develop Plan	Develop strategy (anticipate objections and needs; determine messaging, solutions, and recommendations) Determine approach			
Client Meeting(s)	Schedule initial client meeting Practice, prepare for client appointment Meet with the client (80/20 rule) Team meeting to debrief ID needs, buying initiatives, and drivers, develop solutions			

Action Items		Responsible Person	Timeline	Comments/ Next Steps
Re-Qualify	Confirm urgency, needs, timeline, and next steps with client			
Proposal/ Presentation	Develop presentation/ proposal Practice presentation			
Retain Business/ Cross Sell New Business	Begin planning again			

CHAPTER FLASHBACK

- Create loyal clients. They make a law practice strong and solid.
- The end of a transaction is one of the most opportune times to talk with a client and identify future revenue potential. Ask questions about future needs at this time.
- Visit clients in their offices rather than have meetings in yours.
- Introduce clients and prospects with mutual interests.
- Provide staff with a client service skills-building program annually. Recognize those who go above and beyond the call of duty.
- Client feedback, whether obtained formally or informally, will help you develop your own ways to add value for your clients.

CHAPTER 9

Plan (Again)

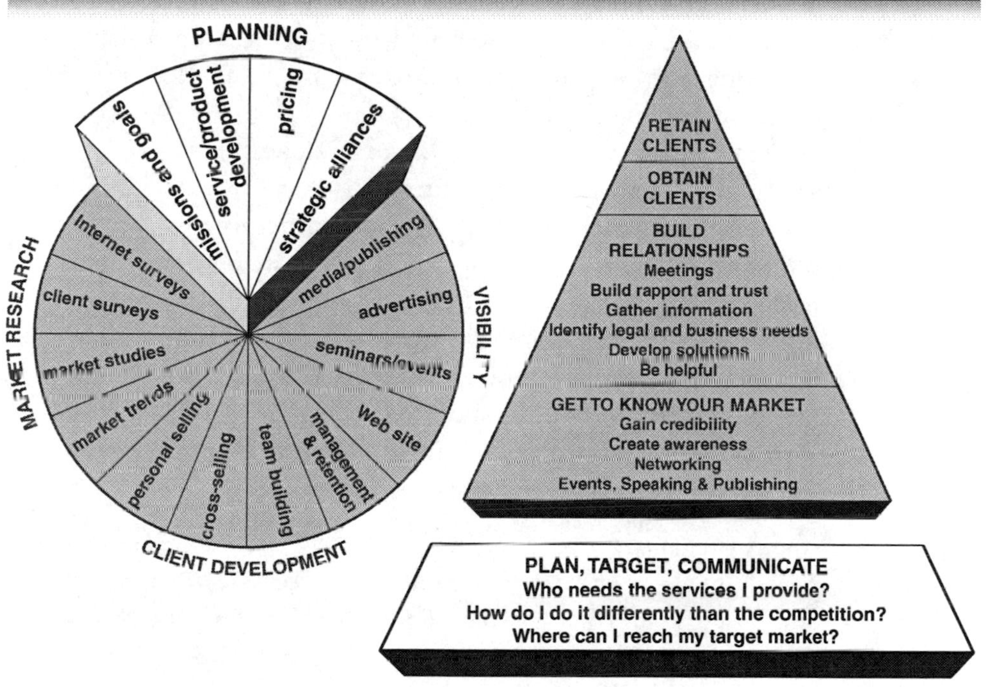

▸ This chapter is a reflection on the fact that the sales cycle is endless. That's right. Now that you've made it through the cycle, start again!

The good news is that you've already created a plan. So, this time, all you need to do is edit it. That is why, in contrast to the first chapter, this one is so short. ◂

QUALIFYING CLIENTS

When you begin planning again, part of what you need to determine is whether you should continue to invest in and keep a particular client. One way to do this is to conduct an annual review. Look at your entire list, and then analyze your clients based on the following questions:

1. How profitable is each client? Every firm has some clients that are highly profitable and some that are not. Before you consider expanding business with a particular client, it is important to prove to yourself that it's worthwhile. Profitability is not the only determinant, however; some clients take longer to be profitable and some are simply less profitable but more enjoyable.
2. How can we add value with top clients? What industry trends will affect the client? What issues will their business face in the next 12–24 months? What is the client trying to accomplish over the next 12–24 months? How can we help the client reach those goals?
3. How much growth potential does each client have? What legal work are we doing now? What legal work are competitors doing that we could handle?
4. How satisfying is it to work with each client? Does the client pay bills on time, or is it a constant battle?

As we stated previously, not all clients are "good" clients. Have the courage to let go the clients who aren't good for you. But if any clients are truly awful, then let them find their own lawyers. Don't pass off an impossible client to anyone you want in your referral network!

PLANNING FOR ACTION

The sales process is one that, if followed successfully, means you get to go back to the beginning. Now you have good habits, checklists, forms, and organizational tools in place. You also have an appreciation for what a plan should be doing for you, which is getting you into action. We have referred to the tendency lawyers have toward "analysis paralysis" and we hope that by this point in your reading, you've gained more of a bias toward action.

The most challenging aspects of personal marketing and selling are to stay disciplined and stay active especially during busy, billable times. If you don't stay active during these times, you will be at a disadvantage when things slow down. If you go for periods of time without taking any action, read the Best Practices in Chapter 10, and enlist the help of mentors or a coach to get and keep you moving. Don't put off investing in your own future.

There are a number of reasons for inaction, from personality type and cultural concerns to financial and structural issues. But at the end of the day, the questions to ask yourself are: Will I take the time to turn my good ideas into action? Will I wisely invest my time in building and maintaining my career?

There's a difference between simple and easy. While incorporating these processes into your practice day to day won't be easy, we have given you hundreds of simple ideas to get you started. Good luck!

CHAPTER FLASHBACK

- The sales cycle is endless.
- Conduct an annual review.
- If you go for periods of time without taking any action, enlist the help of mentors or a coach to get and keep you moving.
- Stay disciplined and keep active.

CHAPTER 10

Best Practices in One Minute

This chapter is designed as a one minute read.

The following tips are designed to be less specific but serve as constant reminders of a simple rule, idea, or tip we've discussed in the book. Bookmark this chapter and refer back to it frequently. It will constantly remind you of what you can do to get more clients and keep the ones you have.

1. It's a long-term process. It takes six to eight contacts with prospects before closing the business. Don't get discouraged and stop communications if you are not hired during the first few interactions. Continue to be helpful.
2. Review your goals and measure progress quarterly. Make adjustments as necessary.
3. Make your introduction about what you do, not who you are. "I'm a real estate lawyer" isn't as effective as "I work with owners and developers in acquisitions and dispositions of real estate." Be clear and crisp; then remember to ask about the other person.
4. Leverage client relationships. Your clients are the best source for new business whether for a new matter or transaction or a referral to a friend/colleague. Ask clients for referrals.
5. Ask smart, open-ended questions and listen. When meeting prospects, practice the "80/20," or "deposition" rule: *80 percent*

of the time: LISTEN. 20 percent of the time: SPEAK AND ASK QUESTIONS. Understand what *this person* thinks his legal need is and address that. Many times, we try to sell a solution to an issue that the clients don't know exists.

6. Find out. Before soliciting business from a new prospect, email your colleagues in the firm to ask if anyone else has relationships with the company and/or person. Email your referral network and other professional service providers. Check news-clipping services and search engines to see if that prospect has been in the press recently.
7. Follow up. Don't leave a meeting without a follow-up timeframe. "When should we touch base again?" "One of our lawyers authored an article on this very topic. I will email it to you when I return to the office." "What are our next steps?" Never leave meetings without offering a valuable follow-up.
8. Send a handwritten note to your client at the end of each matter or transaction.
9. Schedule early and often. Schedule your appointments with prospects early in the morning. The meeting will less likely be canceled, and it won't take too much time away from your billable hour commitments.
10. Keep in contact. Touch base with each of your contacts at least four times a year. Maintain your database! Review and update with new clients, prospects, and referral sources. Make sure contact information stays current. Inactive clients still think of you as their counsel.
11. Get personal. Get to know your clients and prospects personally. Spend time off the clock at their offices and do something that genuinely interests both of you.
12. If you are contacted by a prospect, find out how he/she learned about you or your firm. Track this information each year to inventory what marketing activities are supporting client development.
13. Understand that sales are part process, part patience, and part art. Track the length of your sales cycle (how long it takes from introduction to close) so that you can anticipate the sales time in your particular practice.

14. Just as you would prepare your home for a guest, prepare your office for a client: hangers in the closet, polished conference room tables, comfortable reception area, current periodicals–these are *all* important to the first impression.
15. Dress for success. Although business casual may or may not be the standard, be sure you follow this rule before arriving at a client site in attire that is too casual. Conversely, if your client's business is always casual, they may be more comfortable if you are also less formal. Every client has a different idea of what his/her lawyers should be dressed like.
16. Reception areas are a great place to display reprinted articles you have authored or other news items of interest.
17. Provide business cards to every employee; view all personnel as professional staff.
18. When responding to Requests for Proposals (RFPs), be sure to call the identified contact to discuss and clarify prospect's needs before formally submitting your response. This allows the prospect to briefly "get to know you" and allows you to understand any other issues that are not indicated in the RFP.
19. During travel and commuting time, draft or dictate legal issues articles to be published in community or trade publications.
20. Say "thank you" formally to someone who refers you business; suggestions: a handwritten note or a gift.
21. Schedule time in your calendar (just like an appointment) to touch base with clients you have not spoken to recently.
22. Clients' needs change. Review your brochure and other marketing collateral to be sure you are addressing your current target market. Develop a referral list for services you do not provide, such as financial planning, accounting, etc. Use this list to be helpful to your clients when they have a need for services you can't provide. This also builds valuable relationships with referral sources.
23. Stay in touch with your law school classmates. Other lawyers are a very active referral source.

24. Review your contact list. Have you added those people you have met recently to your list? Have you kept the data current (i.e., change in title, address, company, last name, etc.)?
25. To keep marketing and selling at the forefront of your mind, sign up for the free electronic tip program called Results-Mail™ from Sales Results Inc. at www.salesresults.com or try LSSO (Legal Sales and Services Organization) News at www.legalsales.org.
26. Tickle your calendar to read this chapter again in three months.

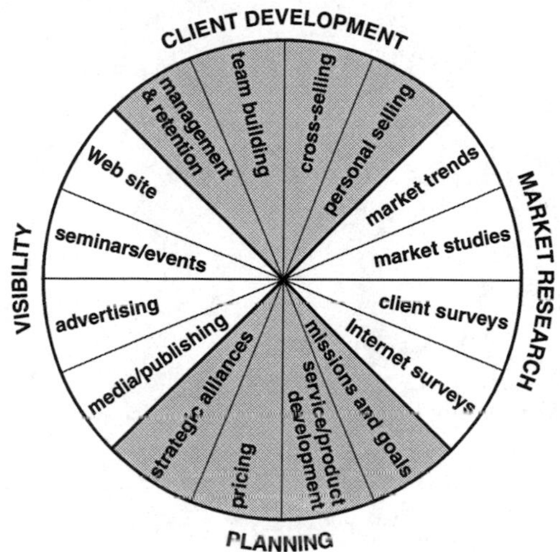

RETAIN CLIENTS

OBTAIN CLIENTS

BUILD RELATIONSHIPS
Meetings
Build rapport and trust
Gather information
Identify legal and business needs
Develop solutions
Be helpful

GET TO KNOW YOUR MARKET
Gain credibility
Create awareness
Networking
Events, Speaking & Publishing

PLAN, TARGET, COMMUNICATE
Who needs the services I provide?
How do I do it differently than the competition?
Where can I reach my target market?

RESOURCES

AUTHORS' TOP PICKS

ASSOCIATIONS

American Bar Association: www.abanet.org

ABA Law Practice Management Section: www.abanet.org/lpm

Association of Legal Administrators (ALA): www.alanet.org

Legal Marketing Association (LMA): www.legalmarketing.org

Legal Sales and Service Organization (LSSO): www.legalsales.org

The National Association for Law Placement (NALP): www.nalp.org

The National Association of Women Lawyers: www.nawl.org

Practice Development Consortium: www.pdclegal.org

BOOKS

AdverSelling: How to Build Stronger Relationships and Close More Sales by Applying 26 Principles from Successful Advertising Campaigns by James Hassett (Brattle Systems, 2005)

Discover Your Sales Strengths: How the World's Greatest Salespeople Develop Winning Careers by Benson Smith & Tony Rutigliano (New York, Warner Books, Inc., 2003)

Endless Referrals (Third edition) by Bob Burg (New York, McGraw-Hill, 2005)

First Among Equals by Patrick J. McKenna and David Maister (New York, The Free Press, 2005)

Fish! by Stephen C., Lundin, Ph.D., Harry Paul and John Christenson (New York, Hyperion, 2000)

How to Get and Keep Good Clients by Jay G. Foonberg (National Academy of Law Ethics, 1994)

How to Get Quoted and Featured in the Media by David M. Freedman and Paula Levis Suita (Chicago, Eminent Publishing, 2006)

How to Do the Interview: Policies, Strategies, and Techniques by David M. Freedman and Paula Levis Suita (Chicago, Eminent Publishing, 2006)

How to Sell More in Less Time With No Rejections by Art Sobczak (Omaha, Business by Phone, 1998)

Inside Outside by Larry Smith (ALM Publishing, 2002)

The Lawyer's Guide to Marketing on the Internet, Third Edition, by Gregory H. Siskind, Deborah McMurray, and Richard P. Klau (Chicago, ABA, 2007)

The Lawyer's Guide to Marketing Your Practice, Second Edition, by James A. Durham and Deborah McMurray (Chicago, ABA, 2003)

Listen Up: Hear What's Really Being Said by Jim Dugger (Florida, American Media Publishing, 1995)

Marketing Success Stories, Second Edition, by Hollis Hatfield Weishar and Joyce K. Smiley (Chicago, ABA, 2004)

Marketing the Law Firm: Business Development Techniques by Sally J. Schmidt (Law Journal Seminars, 1991)

Move the Sale Forward by John Klymshyn (Aberdeen, Silver Lake Publishing, 2003)

Proposals and Responding to RFP by Bob Gahagan

The Quick and Easy Way to Effective Speaking by Dale Carnegie (Vermilion, 1990)

The Rainmaker's Toolkit: Power Strategies for Finding, Keeping, and Growing Profitable Clients by Harry Mills (New York, American Management Association, 2004)

Rain Making: The Professional's Guide to Attracting New Clients by Ford Harding (Bob Adams, Inc., Publishers, 1994)

The Rainmaking Machine: Marketing Planning, Strategy and Management by Phyllis Haserot (New York, Shepard's-McGraw-Hill, 1990)

Rainmaking Made Simple: What Every Professional Must Know by Mark M. Maraia (Professional Services Publishing, 2003)

Raving Fans: A Revolutionary Approach To Customer Service by Ken Blanchard (New York, William Morrow, 1993)

Relationship Selling: The Key to Getting and Keeping Customers by Jim Cathcart (New York, Perigee Trade, 1993)

Selling With Integrity: Reinventing Sales Through Collaboration, Respect, and Serving by Sharon Drew (San Francisco, Berrett-Koehler Publishers, 1997)

Socratic Selling: How to Ask the Questions That Get the Sale by Kevin R. Daley (New York, McGraw-Hill, 1997)

Some Assembly Required by Thom Singer (Danville, New Year Publishing, LLC, 2005)

Speak Like a CEO by Suzanne Bates (New York, McGraw-Hill, 2005)

Spin Selling by Neil Rackham (Gower Publishing Co., 1995)

Stop Selling, Start Partnering: The New Thinking About Finding and Keeping Customers by Larry Wilson (New York, Wiley, 1996)

Super Networking for Sales Pros by Michael Salmon (New Jersey, Career Press, 2005)

Through the Client's Eyes: New Approaches to Get Clients to Hire Again and Again by Henry W. Ewalt (Chicago, ABA Section of Law Practice Management, 1994)

True Professionalism by David Maister (New York, Free Press, 2000)

Trust-Based Selling by Charles H. Green (New York, McGraw-Hill, 2005)

The Trusted Advisor by David Maister, Charles H. Green & Robert M. Galford (New York, Free Press, 2002)

The Women Lawyer's Rainmaking Game by Silvia L. Coulter (Little Falls, Glasser Legal Works, 2004)

52 Ways to Re-Connect, Follow Up & Stay in Touch by Anne Baber and Lynne Waymon (Iowa, Kendall-Hunt, 1994)

104 Activities that Build: Self Esteem, Teamwork, Communication . . . by Alanna Jones (Richland, Rec Room Publishing, 1998)

Internet Resources

The best way to keep up with the world of legal marketing is via the Internet. Things change rapidly, so the most reliable tactic is simply to type a term into Google® and see what comes up.

There are a number of blogs and other sites that you may want to bookmark or subscribe to.

Associate Marketing Mentor: http://pm.typepad.com/associatemarketing/

Bruce Marcus' The Marcus Letter: www.marcusletter.com

Edge International: www.edge.ai

Deborah McMurray's blog about legal marketing and management issues: www.deborahmcmurray.com

Gerry Riskin's Amazing firms, amazing practices: www.gerryriskin.com

Greedy Associates: www.greedyassociate.com

For solos and small firms: www.howtomakeitrain.com

High Tech Marketing for Lawyers: www.htmlawyers.com
www.jimhassett.com
Larry Bodine's Professional Marketing Blog: http://pm.typepad.com
The Law Marketing Portal: www.lawmarketing.com
Legal Biz Dev: www.lawbizdev.com or www.legalbizdev.com
Tom Kane's Legal Marketing Blog: www.legalmarketingblog.com
The Legal Sales and Service Organization: www.legalsales.org
www.raintoday.com
http://rossfishman.wiseadmin.biz
ResultsMail and more from Sales Results Inc.: www.salesresults.com
Dan Hull's What About Clients: www.whataboutclients.com
The WJF Institute: www.wjfinstitute.com

EPILOGUE

TRAINING MANUAL

To help move readers into action we have created a Training Manual. The manual is designed as a leadership tool and a trainer handbook, with instructions to lead discussions, exercises, and workshops with groups of lawyers.

The training manual may be used universally, ranging from groups of lawyers who alternate as discussion leaders to managing partners to in-house professional development administrators. Below is the table of contents from the manual.

INDEX

Selected Books from . . .
THE ABA LAW PRACTICE MANAGEMENT SECTION

The Legal Career Guide: From Law Student to Lawyer, Fourth Edition
By Gary A. Munneke
This is a step-by-step guide for planning a law career, preparing and executing a job search, and moving into the market. Whether you're considering a solo career, examining government or corporate work, joining a medium or large firm, or focusing on an academic career, this book is filled with practical advice that will help you find your personal niche in the legal profession. This book will also help you make the right choices in building resumes, making informed career decisions, and taking the first step toward career success.

Women-at-Law: Lessons Learned Along the Pathways to Success
By Phyllis Horn Epstein
Discover how women lawyers in a wide variety of practice settings are meeting the challenges of competing in an often all-consuming profession without sacrificing their desire for a multidimensional life. Women-at-Law provides a wealth of practical guidance and direction from experienced women lawyers who share their life stories and advice to inspire and encourage others by offering solutions to the challenges—personal and professional. You'll learn that, with some effort, a motivated woman can redirect her career, her home life, and her interests, in the long journey that is a successful life. If you are a law student, a practicing lawyer, or simply a woman considering a career

The Lawyer's Guide to Balancing Life and Work, Second Edition
By George W. Kaufman
This newly updated and revised Second Edition is written specifically to help lawyers achieve professional and personal satisfaction in their career. Writing with warmth and seasoned wisdom, George Kaufman examines how the profession has changed over the last five year, then offers philosophical approaches, practical examples, and valuable exercises to help lawyers reconcile their goals and expectations with the realities and demands of the legal profession. Interactive exercises are provided throughout the text and on the accompanying CD, to help you discover how to reclaim your life. New lawyers, seasoned veterans, and those who have personal relationships to lawyers will all benefit from this insightful book.

How to Build and Manage a Personal Injury Practice, Second Edition
By K. William Gibson
Written exclusively for personal injury practitioners, this indispensable resource explores everything from choosing the right office space to measuring results of your marketing campaign. Author Bill Gibson has carefully constructed this "how-to" manual—highlighting all the tactics, technology, and practical tools necessary for a profitable practice, including how to write a sound business plan, develop an accurate financial forecast, maximize your staff while minimizing costs, and more.

How to Build and Manage an Entertainment Law Practice
By Gary Greenberg
This book addresses a variety of issues critical to establishing a successful entertainment law practice including getting started, preparing a business plan, getting your foot in the door, creating the right image, and marketing your entertainment law practice. The book discusses the basic differences between entertainment law and other types of law practice and provides guidance for avoiding common pitfalls. In addition, an extensive appendix contains sample agreements, forms, letters, and checklists common to entertainment law practitioners. Includes a diskette containing the essential appendix templates, forms and checklists for easy implementation!

How to Build and Manage an Estates Practice
By Daniel B. Evans
Whether you aim to define your "niche" in estates law, or market your estates practice on the Internet, this valuable guide can help you make a practice a success. Chapters are logically organized to lead you through the essential stages of developing your specialty practice and include practical, proven advice for everything from organizing estate planning and trust administration files . . . to conducting estate planning interviews . . . to implementing alternative billing strategies . . . to managing your workload (and staff!). Appendices include such sample documents as: an estate planning fee agreement, an estate administration fee agreement, an estate administration schedule, will execution instructions, and more.

The Successful Lawyer: Powerful Strategies for Transforming Your Practice
By Gerald A. Riskin
Available as a Book, Audio-CD Set, or Combination Package!
Global management consultant and trusted advisor to many of the world's largest law firms, Gerry Riskin goes beyond simple concept or theory and delivers a book packed with practical advice that you can implement right away. By using the principles found in this book, you can live out your dreams, embrace success, and awaken your firm to its full potential. Large law firm or small, managing partners and associates in every area of practice—all can benefit from the information contained in this book. With this book, you can attract what you need and desire into your life, get more satisfaction from your practice and your clients, and do so in a systematic, achievable way.

How to Start and Build a Law Practice, Platinum Fifth Edition
By Jay G Foonberg
This classic ABA bestseller has been used by tens of thousands of lawyers as the comprehensive guide to planning, launching, and growing a successful practice. It's packed with over 600 pages of guidance on identifying the right location, finding clients, setting fees, managing your office, maintaining an ethical and responsible practice, maximizing available resources, upholding your standards, and much more. You'll find the information you need to successfully launch your practice, run it at maximum efficiency, and avoid potential pitfalls along the way. If you're committed to starting—and growing—your own practice, this one book will give you the expert advice you need to make it succeed for years to come.

The Lawyer's Guide to Marketing on the Internet, Second Edition
By Gregory Siskind, Deborah McMurray, and Richard P. Klau
The Internet is a critical component of every law firm marketing strategy—no matter where you are, how large your firm is, or the areas in which you practice. Used effectively, a younger, smaller firm can present an image just as sophisticated and impressive as a larger and more established firm. You can reach potential new clients, in remote areas, at any time, for minimal cost. To help you maximize your Internet marketing capabilities, this book provides you with countless Internet marketing possibilities and shows you how to effectively and efficiently market your law practice on the Internet.

The Lawyer's Guide to Fact Finding on the Internet, Third Edition
By Carole A. Levitt and Mark E. Rosch
Written especially for legal professionals, this revised and expanded edition is a complete, hands-on guide to the best sites, secrets, and shortcuts for conducting efficient research on the Web. Containing over 600 pages of information, with over 100 screen shots of specific Web sites, this resource is filled with practical tips and advice on using specific sites, alerting readers to quirks or hard-to-find information. What's more, user-friendly icons immediately identify free sites, free-with-registration sites, and pay sites. An accompanying CD-ROM includes the links contained in the book, indexed, so you can easily navigate to these cream-of-the-crop Web sites without typing URLs into your browser.

The Lawyer's Guide to Marketing Your Practice, Second Edition
Edited by James A. Durham and Deborah McMurray
This book is packed with practical ideas, innovative strategies, useful checklists, and sample marketing and action plans to help you implement a successful, multi-faceted, and profit-enhancing marketing plan for your firm. Organized into four sections, this illuminating resource covers: Developing Your Approach; Enhancing Your Image; Implementing Marketing Strategies and Maintaining Your Program. Appendix materials include an instructive primer on market research to inform you on research methodologies that support the marketing of legal services. The accompanying CD-ROM contains a wealth of checklists, plans, and other sample reports, questionnaires, and templates—all designed to make implementing your marketing strategy as easy as possible!

The Lawyer's Guide to Creating Persuasive Computer Presentations, Second Edition
By Ann E. Brenden and John D. Goodhue
This book explains the advantages of computer presentation resources, how to use them, what they can do, and the legal issues involved in their use. This revised second edition has been updated to include new chapters on hardware and software that is currently being used for digital displays, and it contains all-new sections that walk the reader through beginning and advanced Microsoft® PowerPoint® skills. Also included is a CD-ROM containing on-screen tutorials illustrating techniques such as animating text, creating zoomed call-out images, insertion and configuration of text and images, and a sample PowerPoint final argument complete with audio, checklists, and help files for using trial presentation software.

30-Day Risk-Free Order Form

Call Today! 1-800-285-2221

Monday–Friday, 7:30 AM – 5:30 PM, Central Time

Qty	Title	LPM Price	Regular Price	Total
_____	The Legal Career Guide: From Law Student to Lawyer, Fourth Edition (5110479)	$ 29.95	$ 34.95	$_______
_____	Women-at-Law: Lessons Learned Along the Pathways to Success (5110509)	39.95	49.95	$_______
_____	The Lawyer's Guide to Balancing Life and Work, Second Edition (5110566)	29.95	39.95	$_______
_____	How to Build and Manage a Personal Injury Practice, Second Edition (5110575)	54.95	64.95	$_______
_____	How to Build and Manage an Estates Practice (5110421)	44.95	54.95	$_______
_____	How to Build and Manage an Entertainment Law Practice (5110453)	54.95	64.95	$_______
_____	How to Start and Build a Law Practice, Platinum Fifth Edition (5110508)	57.95	69.95	$_______
_____	The Lawyer's Guide to Creating Persuasive Computer Presentations, Second Edition (5110530)	79.95	99.95	$_______
_____	The Lawyer's Guide to Fact Finding on the Internet, Third Edition (5110568)	84.95	99.95	$_______
_____	The Lawyer's Guide to Marketing on the Internet, Second Edition (5110484)	69.95	79.95	$_______
_____	The Lawyer's Guide to Marketing Your Practice, Second Edition (5110500)	79.95	89.95	$_______
_____	The Successful Lawyer—Book Only (5110531)	64.95	84.95	$_______
_____	The Successful Lawyer—Audio CDs Only (5110532)	129.95	149.95	$_______
_____	The Successful Lawyer—Audio CDs/Book Combination (5110533)	174.95	209.95	$_______

*Postage and Handling	
$10.00 to $24.99	$5.95
$25.00 to $49.99	$9.95
$50.00 to $99.99	$12.95
$100.00 to $349.99	$17.95
$350 to $499.99	$24.95

**Tax
DC residents add 5.75%
IL residents add 9.00%

***Postage and Handling**	$_______
****Tax**	$
TOTAL	$_______

PAYMENT

❑ Check enclosed (to the ABA)

❑ Visa ❑ MasterCard ❑ American Express

Account Number Exp. Date Signature

Name Firm

Address

City State Zip

Phone Number E-Mail Address

Guarantee

If—for any reason—you are not satisfied with your purchase, you may return it within 30 days of receipt for a complete refund of the price of the book(s). No questions asked!

Mail: ABA Publication Orders, P.O. Box 10892, Chicago, Illinois 60610-0892 ♦ Phone: 1-800-285-2221 ♦ FAX: 312-988-5568

E-Mail: abasvcctr@abanet.org ♦ Internet: http://www.lawpractice.org/catalog

About the CD

The accompanying CD contains checklists, tips, worksheets, and forms from the text of *The Law Firm Associate's Guide to Personal Marketing and Selling Skills.* The files are in Microsoft Word® format.

For additional information about the files on the CD, please open and read the **"readme.doc"** file on the CD.

NOTE: The set of files on the CD may only be used on a single computer or moved to and used on another computer. Under no circumstances may the set of files be used on more than one computer at one time. If you are interested in obtaining a license to use the set of files on a local network, please contact: Director, Copyrights and Contracts, American Bar Association, 321 N. Clark Street, Chicago, IL 60610, (312) 988-6101. **Please read the license and warranty statements on the following page before using this CD.**

CD-ROM to accompany
The Law Firm Associate's Guide to Personal Marketing and Selling Skills

WARNING: Opening this package indicates your understanding and acceptance of the following Terms and Conditions.

READ THE FOLLOWING TERMS AND CONDITIONS BEFORE OPENING THIS SEALED PACKAGE. IF YOU DO NOT AGREE WITH THEM, PROMPTLY RETURN THE UNOPENED PACKAGE TO EITHER THE PARTY FROM WHOM IT WAS ACQUIRED OR TO THE AMERICAN BAR ASSOCIATION AND YOUR MONEY WILL BE RETURNED.

The document files in this package are a proprietary product of the American Bar Association and are protected by Copyright Law. The American Bar Association retains title to and ownership of these files.

License
You may use this set of files on a single computer or move it to and use it on another computer, but under no circumstances may you use the set of files on more than one computer at the same time. You may copy the files either in support of your use of the files on a single computer or for backup purposes. If you are interested in obtaining a license to use the set of files on a local network, please contact: Manager, Publication Policies & Contracting, American Bar Association, 312 N. Clark Street, Chicago, IL 60610, (312) 988-6101.

You may permanently transfer the set of files to another party if the other party agrees to accept the terms and conditions of this License Agreement. If you transfer the set of files, you must at the same time transfer all copies of the files to the same party or destroy those not transferred. Such transfer terminates your license. You may not rent, lease, assign or otherwise transfer the files except as stated in this paragraph.

You may modify these files for your own use within the provisions of this License Agreement. You may not redistribute any modified files.

Warranty
If a CD-ROM in this package is defective, the American Bar Association will replace it at no charge if the defective diskette is returned to the American Bar Association within 60 days from the date of acquisition.

American Bar Association warrants that these files will perform in substantial compliance with the documentation supplied in this package. However, the American Bar Association does not warrant these forms as to the correctness of the legal material contained therein. If you report a significant defect in performance in writing to the American Bar Association, and the American Bar Association is not able to correct it within 60 days, you may return the CD, including all copies and documentation, to the American Bar Association and the American Bar Association will refund your money.

Any files that you modify will no longer be covered under this warranty even if they were modified in accordance with the License Agreement and product documentation.

IN NO EVENT WILL THE AMERICAN BAR ASSOCIATION, ITS OFFICERS, MEMBERS, OR EMPLOYEES BE LIABLE TO YOU FOR ANY DAMAGES, INCLUDING LOST PROFITS, LOST SAVINGS OR OTHER INCIDENTAL OR CONSEQUENTIAL DAMAGES ARISING OUT OF YOUR USE OR INABILITY TO USE THESE FILES EVEN IF THE AMERICAN BAR ASSOCIATION OR AN AUTHORIZED AMERICAN BAR ASSOCIATION REPRESENTATIVE HAS BEEN ADVISED OF THE POSSIBILITY OF SUCH DAMAGES, OR FOR ANY CLAIM BY ANY OTHER PARTY. SOME STATES DO NOT ALLOW THE LIMITATION OR EXCLUSION OF LIABILITY FOR INCIDENTAL OR CONSEQUENTIAL DAMAGES, IN WHICH CASE THIS LIMITATION MAY NOT APPLY TO YOU.